Starting Your Own Business

How to plan, build and manage a successful enterprise

JIM GREEN
3rd edition

How To Books

Published by How To Books Ltd,
3 Newtec Place, Magdalen Road,
Oxford OX4 1RE, United Kingdom.
Tel: (01865) 793806. Fax: (01865) 248780.
email: info@howtobooks.co.uk
www.howtobooks.co.uk

First edition 1995
Second edition 1998
Third edition 2000
Reprinted 2001

British Library Cataloguing in Publication Data
A catalogue record for this book is available from
the British Library

Cover design by Shireen Nathoo Design
Cover image PhotoDisc

Produced for How To Books by Deer Park Productions
Typeset by PDQ Typesetting, Newcastle-under-Lyme
Printed and bound by Cromwell Press, Trowbridge, Wiltshire

NOTE: The material contained in this book is set out in good
faith for general guidance and no liability can be accepted
for loss or expense incurred as a result of relying in particular
circumstances on statements made in the book. Laws and
regulations are complex and liable to change, and readers should
check the current position with the relevant authorities before
making personal arrangements.

Contents

List of Illustrations

Preface

Becoming a successful entrepreneur is not only a rewarding and self-fulfilling experience, it's also a tremendous amount of fun. Many people equate the term entrepreneur with multi-millionaires running international conglomerates. Yet traders just down the street from where you live who make their living from retailing, plumbing, painting and decorating, electrical installation, building, floral arrangement, interior design, child minding, dentistry, chiropody, garden maintenance, insurance, image-making and a host of other things – all are entrepreneurs, and they get as much satisfaction from their enterprises as any multi-millionaires.

Entrepreneurship is an attitude, a whole way of life. When you choose to start your own business you are also choosing to become an entrepreneur, and to begin this new way of life.

Maybe you've already given some thought to striking out on your own but feel that the risks are too great, the timing not right, the economy too bad. You feel you'd never be able to raise the funds, you're too young/old/tired/retired, you're too unemployed/redundant/rejected – you're too whatever.

This book aims to help you decide whether you're right or wrong, whether you have what it takes to strike out on your own and stamp your personality on an enterprise of your very own making.

Let me tell you my own story. It was a cold wet Friday morning in November and for the last time I was walking the short distance from the car park to my little office on the hill. I was feeling my age, the money had almost run out and my wife was just days away from death. Thirty minutes later I had lost my job, my income and my car.

As I trudged through the rain looking for a taxi home I thought, 'You should be cracking up now.' But I wasn't. Instead, I was experiencing an inner peace I'd never felt before, coupled with a fierce determination to fight back.

And fight back I did. I also ceased to worry about *anything* from that day on. It was my personal road to Damascus, the dawn of realisation.

You will find many strands of 'fighting' back throughout these pages. Regardless of your personal circumstances this book will show you how to strike out on your own and get your life going again.

I've been an entrepreneur for a long time. I've won some and I've lost some but I wrote the first edition of this book while I was doing it yet again so that whatever wisdom it might contain would come fresh to the reader from current experience. How, as I complete my revisions for the third edition, I'm still at it: launching a home-based Internet business.

The contents are not about the mechanics of running a business. You won't find any mention of the complexities of the VAT system, how to compile your tax return, what qualities you should be looking for when choosing a solicitor or accountant. There are lots of excellent books around dealing with these matters, including some in this series. This book concentrates on the creative heart of business, on how to develop an exciting enterprise from the original germ of an idea.

If you do decide to become an entrepreneur may good luck and good fortune be yours all the way.

Jim Green

1

Getting Started

Before you make a conscious decision to start out on the exciting journey that leads to entrepreneurship, it's advisable to take stock of yourself. See whether there are any mental blocks standing in your way, blocks that might hold you back in your endeavours. Identify these right now and get to work immediately on eradicating them.

WHAT'S HOLDING YOU BACK?

Something must be holding you back, or you wouldn't even have read this far.

I didn't spot my own mental blocks in time and it cost me my first successful enterprise. In my case it could be summed up as the mid-life crisis. For many of us it arrives at 40-something, for some earlier and for the real tough nuts, early 60s as retirement looms. In my own case it hit me like a thunderbolt at 50.

I was founder, chairman, managing director and majority shareholder of a highly successful advertising agency (lightning does strike twice). Blue chip accounts were our stock-in-trade. Many of them were institutional accounts where the money was safe, you always got paid on time, and you would have had to murder the chairman or his wife to lose the business.

Yet, the business I lost – not the individual accounts but the business I had conceived as a whole, worked long hours to build and for which I had spurned a substantial offer to sell just months before my dénouement. To this day I still have no idea why I turned down that offer because in the end I was relieved to hand over my company to a conglomerate for one pound sterling (I've still got it) just to get rid of the hassle and the £100,000 overdraft. Or so I thought at the time.

Why did I lose my business?

For years I asked myself that question daily and failed to come up with the real answer. The reason was that I was looking in all the wrong places.

- I blamed it on the hassle. (*Untrue* – I loved the hassle.)

- I blamed it on the overdraft. (*Untrue* – the business was solid, the overdraft manageable.)

- I blamed it on key management. (*Untrue* – they all contributed something to the business.)

- I blamed it on domestic pressures. (*Untrue* – although my dear late wife had been stricken by an irreversible illness, she was coping better than me at the time.)

- I blamed it on Old John Barleycorn. (*Untrue* – I ended up in counselling only to find that this wasn't the root cause.)

So what really went wrong?

The truth came to me quietly that day I trudged through the rain looking for a taxi and the answer was the key to the inner peace I was also to discover. I had simply *given* it all way.

At the age of 50, with a successful business, substantial personal cash reserves, a small mansion, three prestige cars, I just blew it. In short, I lost my confidence and ran away. Why?

- *I simply wasn't ready for success.*

Not only did I lose my business, my livelihood, my personal fortune, I was also subjected to a seven year investigation by the Inland Revenue which I wouldn't wish upon anyone (they were so thorough in their endeavours, they ended up *refunding* me over £14,000).

LEARNING TO HANDLE SUCCESS

When do you learn to handle success? Easy. Just as soon as you work out what's stopping you. If you happen to be 20 when you crack this, so much the better, but for many it takes a little longer to face up to the truth.

So what ails you? Now's the time to find out, evaluate the situation and get your life going again. Could it be one or other of the elements of the modern version of the three 'Rs' (redundancy, retirement, rejection)? Is unemployment getting you down? Are you fed up hearing people tell you you're too old? Does everyone say you're too young? Or are you just stuck in a rut?

OVERCOMING THE MENTAL BLOCKS

Let's examine each mental block to see how it might affect your particular circumstances.

Are you finding redundancy tough to handle?

Redundancy is rotten, isn't it? One day you're one of the crowd, the next you're out on your butt in the freezing cold. The employer may give you a sweetener but it's rarely generous. It soon disappears on urgent calls from the bank manager, mortgage lender and sundry other claimants. Instead of staying home feeling miffed, wouldn't it be more satisfying to get out there and *do* something about your future? After all, you *have* got one.

Has retirement come too early for you?

If you fail to plot the route through your late years accurately, you may be in for some heavy weather ahead. Some people make the mistake of retiring far too early, have lots of cash, lots of time on their hands... and a terrible feeling of frustration. Even if you're fit and well, you'll still need an outlet for your energy. What better than something of a commercial nature?

If you don't need the profits, you can always give them away to a deserving cause. Read on.

Is constant rejection getting you down?

I've been there many times. After I lost my business I worked for several years as a home-based marketing consultant and was doing pretty well until the recession began to bite in October 1990 when I suddenly became a dispensable luxury to my clients. They could no longer afford me and day by day I received 'Dear John' letters. However, one of these clients seemed to think I still had something to offer. He put me on his payroll. That lasted twelve months, then he went spectacularly bust.

Following a period of totally unprofitable activity I sold advertising space as a self-employed rep for a national publishing concern. After a while they offered me full-time employment as a contracts negotiator. Then they got rid of me, and their top management, as they too proceeded to go bust in an even more spectacular way. Not very impressive, is it? Read on.

Do you feel helpless in unemployment?
Then for your own peace of mind, *don't*. There's a vast amount of practical help to be found once you start looking in the right places. I'm not being crass when I say this. I've been unemployed and managed to fight my way out of it once I learned to look in the right places for help. Read on.

Who says you're too old?
No one has yet dared say that straight to my face but I'm fairly sure many have thought so. So what? They're wrong and I can prove it.

Who says you're too young?
They're wrong too, so wrong. The future of the country lies squarely in the hands of its young citizens and you are *never* too young to start learning your trade as an entrepreneur.

Are you just stuck in a rut?
Maybe you are currently in a well paid, secure salaried position but bored out of your skull. Then *do something about it*.

FIGHTING BACK

Finding out what is really holding you back often takes some time, and a good deal of soul searching. Again, the answer may come to you in a flash. In my case it happened the day my employment was terminated. After years of looking in all the wrong places, suddenly everything clicked into place. Within the space of a few hours I had not only identified my own particular core problem but was fighting my way back to recovery.

- The gathering clouds of personal tragedy had brought me the answer. *Worry* was what had been holding me back. The route to recovery was to create a business of my own in the industry I had just been dismissed from and to develop that business free from the fear of worry.

This soul destroying emotion had been eating away at me all my life: not overtly in what I said or did, but subconsciously before I even got around to thought, speech or deed. Worry was my addiction and I simply couldn't leave it alone. It had enshrouded all the plans that had gone before and as a result tainted their development.

Building the path to recovery

I was good, *very* good, at what I did in the industry I had been thrown out of earlier that day: contracts negotiation. I also had a working knowledge of all the other aspects in which I had not been actively involved. With over 30 years' hands-on experience in the advertising industry, I reckoned I had at my fingertips all the makings of a successful publisher.

I determined there and then – without capital or resources – to create my own publishing business and to do so free from the fear factor. Not helping you much all of this is it? Bear with me a little longer.

I decided to put the matter of lack of capital and resources on the back burner meantime and to concentrate on the immediate essentials of creating a basic plan initially for survival, then for success.

My shopping list comprised the following:

- Sign on the UBO for the first time in my life.

- Inform all of my previous clients of my intention to start again on my own.

- Find some money to live on.

- Get myself mobile again.

- Locate a cost-free training course on information technology.

- Create the beginnings of my business plan.

- Look again at personal financing for my enterprise.

- Discover if I had any friends who might consider investing.

- Establish the route to public sector funding.

- Brush up on my entrepreneurial skills.

How I achieved all ten of these initial goals and how their development contributed to my master plan is the basic subject matter of the chapters to follow. My hope is to offer you an insight into what it takes to become an entrepreneur. I did it, and so too can you.

What's held you back so far?

Now that you've heard my confession, let's have a quick recap on what might be *your* mental block to launching your very own enterprise.

Too old?   _____
Too young?   _____
Too tired?   _____
Too retired?   _____
Too broke?   _____
Too redundant?   _____
Too rejected?   _____
Too much to hope for? _____

However you may view yourself right now, there's no telling how far you can go if you really put your mind to it. For the moment, please take my word for this statement. Later, if you persevere, you'll discover the truth of it for yourself.

Too old?
Says who? You're really only as old as you have a mind to be.

Too young?
Rubbish. Go for it. You may not get a second chance.

Too tired?
Then wake up. Creative activity is happening all around you. Join in.

Too retired?
Then start over again and get back in the driver's seat.

Too broke?
So was I. In Chapter 4 I'll tell you how to remedy the situation.

Too redundant?
So no one's ever going to employ you again. So what? Get started

and hire yourself. It'll be the best job and the best boss you've ever had.

Too rejected?
There's only one way to get rid of it. *Forget it.* But only after you've forgiven those who are doing the rejecting. They don't know your side of it and, even if they did, they probably wouldn't understand.

Too much to take on board?
Can't be or you wouldn't still be with me.

You'll need a plan before you start
The beginnings of my plan was the little shopping list outlined above. Perhaps it might be no bad thing if you were to do likewise. Just jot down the basic things you have to do to get yourself going again.

Let's see how I got on ticking off the initial items on my list.

Signing on
That was an experience. The young lady behind the desk enquired about the occupation I'd just lost, then took a quizzical look at me as she said: 'Oh, there's not much call for that around here. Shall I put you down for clerical vacancies?' Charming.

Informing my clients
Easy. I rattled out a standard letter on my ailing Amstrad, personalised it, told everyone the truth and asked them to keep the kettle warm as I'd be back on their doorstep with my own business within the year.

Finding the money to live on
Not so easy. My visit to the UBO established the fact that I was not entitled to unemployment benefit. I had insufficient NI contributions, having been in a full-time job for less than two years (I was previously self-employed). So for the next six months I lived on Social Security. It didn't bother me. I'd paid plenty into the system for 40 years prior.

The DSS money was topped up by £1,000 I raised from selling personal odds and ends, and following extensive correspondence with the Inland Revenue I managed to obtain a tax refund. It was very tight for six months but I managed somehow.

LAUNCH PAD

1 Find an idea

2 Get some cash together

3 Think about a trading name

4 Research the market

5 Study the competition

6 Write a business plan

7 Locate a training programme

8 Choose a partner

9 Investigate potential funders

10 Talk to the bank manager

11 Source initial equipment

12 ......

Fig. 1. Getting on the launch pad.

Getting mobile again
I had no spare cash and HP was out of the question, so I hawked a diamond ring I'd bought my wife many years before. It had cost £5,000. Mappin & Webb in their generosity and my desperation gave me £1,150 for it. That allowed me to invest in a little red Lada which gave me excellent service for the next half year.

Cost-free training
The UBO were less than helpful. Too old to qualify for free training, they reckoned. So I bounced around in my Lada from one training house to another without much success. Finally I came across one where the chief trainer gave me the age limit for recruits with his first breath. I sawed five years off my age and was admitted that very afternoon to an Information Technology Course. The 'training' was non-existent but I spent the time poring over manuals and engaging in interactive, tutorial dialogue with a stream of delightful young Americans. The course ran for 13 weeks, five days a week and was excellent value at 0 per cent APR. I was computer literate at the end. A few months later I received a cheque for £25 for being top student (that means the one that got a job).

Maybe the first few items of your initial list will show up something like this:

1. Find an idea.

2. Write a business plan.

3. Find some seed capital.

4. Source the mainstream finance needed.

5. [and so on].

CHECKING YOUR READINESS

What's *really* holding you back?

- Are you willing to do something about it?

- Are you worried about becoming really successful?

- Are you still worried about being considered too old or too young?

- Are you still worried that your unemployment status will count against you?

- Are you bothered about feeling broke?
- Are you ready to draw up a plan?

CASE STUDIES

Tom's first steps to freedom

Tom was made redundant nine months ago. He had been suffering from acute depression until recently when he finally made his mind up to do something about it. Tom had often thought about going into business for himself; since it now seemed clear that no one else was likely to offer him a job in the near future, he concentrated all his efforts on planning the launch of his own enterprise. Tom was a printer by trade, so a small jobbing print shop was what he set his sights on.

Tom had taken his first two steps on the journey towards entrepreneurship: he faced up to what was troubling him and he started to make a plan.

Paul and Hazel team up

Paul is 19 and his girlfriend Hazel is his junior by one year. Just weeks after leaving school Paul secured a job as an apprentice cook in the canteen of the local District Council offices. He loved his job but because of cutbacks (or so they said at the time) he was made redundant on his 18th birthday. He hasn't worked since.

Hazel on the other hand has never had a job since leaving school, but not for the want of trying. She hasn't been wasting time though. She's attended several youth training schemes including one on business administration which she found most enjoyable.

On the way back from the Job Centre one day, Hazel stopped in her tracks, tapped Paul on the shoulder and said,

'Hey, we could do that. We could start our own business.'

'Do what?' said Paul.

Hazel pointed to a mobile fast food shop on the other side of the street.

'Don't be daft. We don't know anything about running a business and anyway, we've got no money.'

'We could always get some. We wouldn't need much and my dad is forever saying you can always get money for a good idea.'

'Fat lot of good it's done him, he's still on the dustcart.'

'But we could do it. You can cook and I know about business administration ...'

John and Colin pool their ideas

Neither John (55) nor Colin (52) needed to work for an income but what they did need was a job. They had both taken early retirement from well paid occupations with index linked pensions.

Retirement was great to begin with, but as time wore on boredom set in. The days were a drag and both men were really frustrated.

One afternoon John and Colin compared notes on the bowling green and decided that they still had plenty to offer and what they needed was a meaningful outlet for their energies. After tossing a few ideas around they came up with the notion of supplying their services to the community...but how?

ACTION POINTS

1. List any mental blocks you feel may be holding you back in thinking seriously about setting up on your own.

2. Focus on the one mental block that may be the key to the others.

3. Try drawing up a strategy to overcome this.

4. Make a stab at an initial plan of action.

5. Select the most difficult aspect and write down how you intend to resolve this.

2

Finding a Good Idea

You'll need a really hot idea to get your enterprise going, but that's no great problem. There are hundreds of great business ideas, if you know where and how to look for them.

LOOKING RIGHT IN FRONT OF YOU

- Which subject did you enjoy most at school?

- Were you good at what you did when you were in full-time employment?

- Did you enjoy what you did for a living?

- If you are currently in employment, are you happy doing what you do?

- Could you do it successfully without any supervision?

- Are there aspects of your work you could improve upon if only someone asked for your advice?

- Does what you do (or did) make money for your employer?

- Is there still a market demand for the product or service?

Moving ahead by changing direction

Think, too, about how you might use your experience in launching out in business but taking a body swerve in direction – poacher turned gamekeeper. I did just that; for many years I had bought advertising space in large quantities for my clients. Then I changed to selling it in even larger quantities to subsidise the production of my publications. The experience gained in one aspect of the industry paid off handsomely on the other side of the fence. You might well find a similar application for your experience.

CASHING IN ON CHANGE

The economy is crying out for entrepreneurs of all ages, irrespective of social standing and net worth. The days of conglomerate inward investment as a safe route to economic progression are over. What's needed now are thousands of home-grown well thought out start-ups to foster recovery and engender the re-growth of our economy. The whole national and international economy is changing at a huge rate, affecting every market for private and public sector products and services. Business opportunities are everywhere.

Maybe you don't want to go back to what you did, maybe you have no idea what you'd like to do or maybe you just want to keep your options open. But here are some starting points for coming up with ideas.

Entrepreneurship training programmes

Waste no time in approaching your local Training & Enterprise Council (TEC), Enterprise Agency, Enterprise Trust (they vary in name according to region). Ask for details of which programmes they sponsor relating to **entrepreneurship**. These programmes are orchestrated by commercial concerns but the high running costs are met by central and local government agencies (a measure of official concern about the absolute necessity for growth).

Apart from being the best option for sourcing business propositions that are thoroughly researched, tried, tested *and* work, these programmes will also provide you with a real grounding in the **skills** you'll need to run a business.

ACQUIRING COMMERCIAL SKILLS

Here's a list of the topics to be found in a typical prospectus:

Team building
New business planning
Markets and market selection
Product identification
Support systems for start-ups
Financial planning
Sourcing public sector financing
Sourcing private sector financing
Sourcing proven ideas
Legal aspects

Producing your business plan
Launching and managing your new venture

The particular course I happened upon was called 'The Entrepreneurship Programme' and was superbly run by my now good friends Andy McNab who initiated the programme, Will McKee, Les McKeown (entrepreneurs in their own right) and Dennis Murphy, programme manager par excellence. They're not paying me to say nice things about them. But I owe them all. The 26 week course cost me just £150 and I reckon I got 100 times that value out of it.

Do yourself a favour and enquire now.

WORKING ON YOUR SELF-ESTEEM

You won't find age, social standing or net worth a barrier. The only thing that might debar you is low self-esteem. Get working on that now if you think you have a problem.

All you will have to do is show willing to learn and participate with your fellow entrepreneurs on the course. You should be at a real advantage because this book will give you a practical insight into many of the topics you'll encounter.

CHOOSING A TRADING NAME

This is a vital question you will need to address as soon as possible. List as many ideas as you can before deciding on the name your enterprise is to trade under. Getting it right from the start is essential – you don't want to have to change it after a few months or a year. There are a few house rules to become familiar with before proceeding further. In essence, the ideal trading name should meet these five requirements:

Five guidelines
1. No more than seven letters in the composition of the core word in the title, preferably five.

2. No more than three syllables in pronunciation of the core word, preferably two.

3. The name must look *and* sound right.

4. It must fit the purpose of the enterprise.

5. It must be legally acceptable.

Let's examine each of these points in detail.

Five to seven letters
Why? Because the shorter the better for memorability *eg* FOCUS (5), HABITAT (7). Look at the big names in retailing: COMET, ARGOS, INDEX, VOGUE, B&Q, HOMEBASE. Keep it short and simple. As long it complies with the other four guidelines you should be on a winner.

Two to three syllables
Why? Your trading name must roll off the tongue as sweetly as honey off a spoon, for example Fo-cus (2), Hab-i-tat (3). Avoid tongue twisters at all costs if your name is to be famous one day. There are some well known exceptions but none of them breaks your jaw. MARKS & SPENCER (13 letters, 4 syllables) but most people say M&S or Marks & Sparks. LITTLEWOODS (10 letters but only 3 syllables). McDONALDS (9 letters, 3 syllables).

Sounding and looking right
Get 1 and 2 right and your chosen name will sound right. But it's got to look good, too, and lend itself to graphic development. That's why a maximum of seven letters is desirable. It will be easier to put it into a graphic context.

Fitness to purpose
This seems obvious enough and hardly worth comment, but while driving through Cheshire I happened upon three examples which blew away this particular guideline:

> Mistletoe Heating & Ventilation
> Thistledown Hydraulics
> Verabill Transport

What does Mistletoe have in common with heating and ventilation or Thistledown with hydraulics? Does anyone know? As for Vera and Bill (bless 'em) why don't they find another name. How about 'Stagecoach'? (Sorry, too late – this beautifully simple, apposite tag has already made Ann Gloag rich and famous.)

Whatever, avoid generics like Acme and Ajax. They have become hackneyed and convey nothing.

Using your own name

This is quite acceptable and makes a lot of sense if you're setting up as a consultant of one kind or another. But keep it simple. Not 'Charles A Farley Marketing Services', but 'Farley Marketing', for example, using the core words to best effect.

Legally acceptable

When you've finally decided on a name, make sure that (a) it conforms to legal requirements, and (b) no one else is already using it. You can easily do this yourself (by completing the necessary forms and paying a small fee) or by instructing your solicitor. Don't despair if you discover that someone else is already trading under the name of your choice.

The trade classification may be different. I wanted to call my company Focus Publishing but the search indicated another company with that name. Further investigation confirmed they were graphic designers whereas my business is publishing. All I had to do was effect a slight change, so I opted for Focus Publishing International as it had always been my intention to have the company trading overseas in due course.

There's a lot in a name. Get it right from the beginning: it could become expensive to change it later.

CHECKING YOUR READINESS

- Where is the first place you will look for an idea for your enterprise?

- Why would you say start-ups are so important to the economy?

- Where can you learn to become an entrepreneur?

- Why is good self-esteem so valuable? Will you do something about yours if it's at a low ebb?

- Why is it vital to get the right trading name? How many letters and syllables will yours contain?

- When could it be okay to use your own name?

- Will the name fit the purpose of your enterprise?

- Will it be legally acceptable?

CASE STUDIES

Tom finds a training programme

Although Tom was 90 per cent certain that he wanted to open a print shop he decided to keep his options open and began hunting for a government sponsored entrepreneurship programme. He didn't have far to look because within days he spotted a full page advertisement in his local paper giving complete details of the prospectus, starting date and entry requirements.

Tom wasted no time in applying. The following week he attended an interview for selection. He was pleasantly surprised at how well it went. He seemed to be just the sort of chap they wanted to recruit and although he had to answer many questions not once did the interviewer ask Tom for his age. Tom was 49 and reckoned that might be against him. He was wrong.

By being selected for this entrepreneurship training programme (although he didn't appreciate the fact at the time) Tom was going to benefit greatly from the commercial skills he would acquire and the opportunity of seeking out a partner for his new enterprise.

Hazel's dad 'weighs in'

'But no one will take us seriously,' said Paul.

'Yes, they will if we've got a plan,' replied Hazel.

'What kind of plan can we come up with to raise some capital? Anyway we've got nothing to start with but our dole money.'

'I can write us a plan, I learned how to do that on the business administration course and dad's promised us £500 to get us going. I talked it over with him last night and he thinks it's a great idea.'

'Business must be booming on the dust...'

Opportunity knocks for John and Colin

The day following their chat on the bowling green John and Colin made an appointment to visit the local Social Services department to see whether there was any call for their idea of community service. Much to their surprise they found there was. One of the biggest problems in the area was locating a reliable concern who would contract to ferry elderly and disabled citizens to and from various social gatherings the department had arranged on a weekly basis. It was recommended at the meeting that John and Colin should visit the Local Enterprise Trust to enquire whether there was any assistance on offer for such a project.

ACTION POINTS

1. Write a brief statement on what you're really good at. How would you enjoy doing it for a living? Could you make money out of it in a business of your own?

2. Assuming that you do not wish to set up a business in the precise industry in which you gained your experience, how could you put that experience to good use in a different direction?

3. Start finding out as much as you can about courses sponsored by Central Government which specialise in 'Setting Up Your Own Business'.

4. Make a list of the commercial skills you would like to acquire.

5. Think of six possible trading names you could use.

3

Creating a Winning Business Plan

You can't start too early creating your plan for achievement. Start *now*. Don't even wait until you've settled on an idea. That may take a little time and no bad thing either. Best to get it right from the beginning. 'But how can I start writing a plan for my business when I'm not absolutely sure yet what I'm going to be doing?'

Fair comment, but what you can do is to *plan* for your Plan.

PLANNING AHEAD

No one really likes writing reports, and that basically is what your business plan will be, a report. It will be a report to keep you focused on your goal, a report which will gradually shape up as the means of impressing investors, raising the necessary capital and turning your idea into reality.

The first thing is to learn how to create a winning plan, a plan that is well researched and grows in value each time you work on it.

Get all the help you can in the beginning. There are some very good books on the subject. If you've never written a business plan for yourself before, I would recommend you invest in a copy of *The 24 Hour Business Plan* by Ron Johnson, published by Hutchinson Business Books at just under £20. It is excellent value, but I'm not suggesting you attempt to write your plan in 24 hours, and neither does the author. Read the book through once and then use it as a constant reference manual as you progress your own plan. It will lead you gently through the intricacies of composing a *winning* plan and give you a grounding in the structure required. If you would rather use a paperback, see Matthew Record's *Preparing a Business Plan* (How To Books).

Focusing on the end result

Developing your business plan should be fun. It will get the creative juices flowing and keep your mind focused on the ultimate goal:

turning your idea into a practical, profitable enterprise of your own.

Even if you haven't finally settled on an idea yet, you'll find that as your learning curve accelerates so too will a decision on the idea that will change your life for the better. The inspiration will soon flow.

A winning plan calls for a high degree of introspection. As you progress you'll find yourself facing up to reality quite readily. When you start committing your thoughts to paper the good, the bad and the ugly aspects of any business idea come to light fairly quickly. This can prove unsettling at first but you'll soon find that you are addressing the negative factors with increasing confidence and vigour. Certain aspects will call for an immediate re-think, further research or perhaps total rejection. Now's the time to find out and put matters right. There will be no scope for dummy runs once you begin trading. Basically, that's what will make your plan a winner: examining, honing and polishing all the components before you fix them firmly into place.

Remember, if you're less than 100 per cent convinced about the finished article, what chance will you have of impressing potential investors?

Example: Focus Publishing International
For the record, I started to put my business plan together the very day I was made redundant and worked solidly on it every day for seven months. Although I'm no accountant I provided initial projections for cash flow and profit & loss spanning three successive years. It will really pay you to do this even though you are rather unsure of many of the figures. Use trial and error. Practice makes perfect, and you can always call on professional help later on.

When I applied to join the 'Entrepreneurship Programme' I did so with three key aims in mind:

- to brush up my entrepreneurial skills
- to discover a route to public sector funding
- to find a management accountant to be a partner and shareholder in my enterprise.

I was successful in all three of my aims and it was my partner-to-be who restructured my rough financial projections into a meaningful, attractive proposition for potential investors. But he had the initial raw material to work on and only I could have produced that. I knew the business.

MAKING SURE THE PLAN IS YOURS

Whatever shape your winning plan eventually takes, make sure it's got *your* hand on it. You may need help with the overall structure and that's OK but don't be tempted (even if you have the money) to rush out and assign all this hard work to a management accountancy practice specialising in the preparation of business plans (not unless your idea has enormous investment potential). If not, you're liable to get a pull-down menu version adjusted to suit the profile of your idea – and you won't get much change out of £2,000.

It's your baby and you must see it through all the way. It's you and *your* team who will one day have to put the plan into practical effect: not a professional adviser.

YOUR BLUEPRINT FOR SUCCESS

The plan you are conceiving for your business is your blueprint for success. Plans are great things. They show you where you're going, what to do and how to do it when you get there. Make no mistake, your business plan isn't just designed to get you started and raise some working capital. It's going to be around for a long time and you'll want to review and update it regularly to take account of the unexpected twists and turns along the way. That's the beauty of it. When you have a plan, you can legislate for change. Without one you're sunk. You'll be an explorer in a jungle without a map.

While no two business plans are alike, they all have similarities in structure. The temptation can be strong (you'll find this out very quickly) to crash on and produce a tome as thick as *War and Peace*. Avoid this temptation. The fewer the pages in your final document the better. A dozen or two may suffice. Quantity will never impress an investor, it's the quality of the idea they measure together with their conception of how likely you will be to turn it into a reality.

The format you must work to is simplicity itself. You deal in turn with each of the component parts in a logical and progressive manner, much as you will do when you're actually putting them all together at the outset of your enterprise.

Putting the pieces together
Here's your initial scheme. Ironically, it begins with the one exception to the advice in the paragraph immediately above.

Structuring the executive summary

You will write this only on completion of the entire plan but it must appear at the very beginning. Why? Because potential investors are unlikely to progress further in their reading unless you give them an immediate 'handle' on what you and your idea are all about. This is also the most difficult section to write and usually takes a few attempts before you can satisfactorily mould it. It shouldn't be any longer than a couple of pages so a great deal of thought has to go into what headings stay in and what ones are left out. No one knows the subject matter better than you. Only you can write it.

Your management team expertise

If you're going to use your plan to raise capital, you'll need to give details of the status, qualifications and experience of your key personnel. It is extremely difficult to attract mainstream investment nowadays for a one-man band. It's possible, but the conditions are restrictive. However, don't be put off. Your initial team could acceptably comprise yourself and one other person: spouse, partner, boyfriend, girlfriend, son, daughter, niece, nephew or, as in my own case, an equity partner.

Your concept

You understand your business idea inside out but does anyone else have a clue what it's all about? Summarise your concept in writing on just one page. Explain in detail exactly what it is. Leave emotion out of it. Stick to the facts.

How your concept works

Many good business ideas fail to get past the starting gate simply because the originator can't or won't elaborate on how the idea works in practice. Once again a single page will suffice, but be precise. In my experience, the inclusion of a simple diagram or flowchart works wonders.

Your business objectives

Your objectives must be detailed, well thought out and thoroughly researched. They should include not only the objectives for your embryo enterprise but also your own personal aspirations for the venture and how you plan to achieve the goals you've set. You'll want to list them as they apply to the short, medium and long term. There's nothing difficult or mysterious about any of this, it's simply a matter of doing it.

What do you know about the market?

You'll need to do some research before you pen this section (even though you reckon you know all there is to know about your market). Markets and market trends change constantly and rapidly, sometimes overnight. Into which sector or sub-sector of the market will your product/service fit? Will it be sold on through conventional channels or will it require specialised distribution? These are just some of the questions you'll be answering.

Researching the competition

There's no show without Punch and where there's no competition, there's unlikely to be any business around either. Find out who your competitors are. Which of them are the strongest in your catchment area? Discover all you can about them and record it faithfully in your plan – even if some of it scares you.

Describe your product

Describe in detail – in not more than one page – exactly what your product or service is. Summarise where it differs from similar propositions, what the benefits are to the end consumer, and why you believe you're on a winner.

Packaging your proposition

Here's where you wrap 'Concept', 'Methodology' and 'Product/Service' into the unique package you'll be offering your customers. Even one slight improvement on what the competition offers might be sufficient to give you an early edge. Will it be discounting, overall pricing policy, unique marketing, or what?

Evolving your sales policy

The marketing plan for your idea will determine your sales policy and whether you require to invest in a sales force. Will you be selling through wholesalers, agents, retailers, off-the-page or door-to-door?

Marketing your business

A great deal of rubbish is spouted about this key business function and usually by people who should know better (see Chapter 6). Suffice to say, keep your marketing simple and relevant to your idea. There's no mystique about the subject.

Your unit production/sales forecast

Whether you're planning to manufacture or to provide a service,

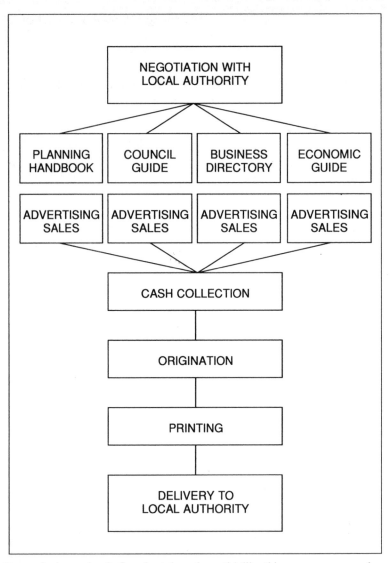

By producing a simple flowchart (or schematic) like this one, you can make it easier for others to understand what your venture is all about. It works best if you can illustrate an element of uniqueness *ie* in this example the cash is collected *before* pressing the button on producing the product.

Fig. 2. A typical format for a business plan.

you'll still want to complete this section: the number of knobblewockers you intend to knock out weekly – or the number of assignments you are forecasting to complete.

Your production costs
Again, whether manufacturing or supplying a service, you'll be incurring production costs and, before you get to your bottom line, you'll have to make estimates for them.

The strengths and weaknesses of your idea
Even though you believe you're on a winner, you may just have re-invented the wheel. There are bound to be some weaknesses in any proposed new operation. Jot them down as well as the strengths. If you don't do it now, some potential investor will do it for you just when you least expect it.

GETTING HELP FROM THE PUBLIC SECTOR

When you get around to seeking financial backing for your project, you'll be asked to make out a case for it. Here's just the place to start.

- Will you be creating additional jobs in your area?

- Would you be prepared to recruit unemployed labour?

- Would you offer training?

- Do you envisage doing business outwith your local economy?

If you can answer 'Yes' to these four questions, you'll be a prime candidate for public sector assistance by way of grants and/or 'soft' loans. More of this in Chapter 4.

Funding your enterprise
You will be demonstrating projections over three successive years for cash flow, profit & loss and balance sheet. If you're not an accountant, call in some expert help. Whatever, be honest and practical. Don't delude yourself or tell porkies. Why funders require fantasy forecasting for years two and three I'll never know but they insist on it.

Useful appendix/appendices
A very useful section into which you can house all the other pieces of back-up information that don't seem to fit in too well elsewhere (CVs, price lists, budget workings etc).

GETTING HELP FROM THE BANKS

Contact the Small Business Adviser at your nearest main clearing bank branch and request a copy of their respective Business Start-Up Packs. Barclays and Natwest are particularly good. I cannot recommend these superbly constructed documents too highly. Study the contents assiduously and they will provide you with an easily digestible insight into all you need to know before putting your plan together. They approach the exercise from different angles and by reading both you'll benefit from two sets of expertise. It's a pity they're not always so forthcoming at handing out the cash but more on that subject later and how to deal with it.

It sounds like a great deal of hard work, this blueprint for success. It is but there's no other way. Once you get started, you'll find your imagination taking off; all sorts of things that didn't make too much sense before will now start falling into place. Try it, you'll be surprised how good you will become at it.

CHECKLIST

● Plan ahead for your business plan.

● Focus on the end result.

● Write the plan all by yourself.

● Summarise the content and position it accordingly.

● Explain exactly how your business idea works in practice.

● Describe your business objectives.

● Define the marketplace.

● Research the competition.

- Produce a clear description of your product or service.

- Describe the key elements of your sales policy.

- Develop a plan to market your enterprise.

- Summarise both the strengths and weaknesses of your idea.

- Make out a case for public sector assistance.

- Show how you will fund your business.

- Describe the market, its characteristics and current trends.

- Show precisely where your product or service fits in.

- If it slots into a particular niche, describe this sub-sector.

CONSTRUCTING YOUR 'BLUEPRINT FOR SUCCESS'

You can't start too soon preparing the business plan that will crystallise your thoughts and bring your idea to the attention of potential investors. Imagine the overall template as the trunk of a pine tree with the bold headings as branches and the bullet points as pine needles. Here's how it works:

Executive summary
- Brief description of the business.
- Target market segment.
- What makes your enterprise different from competitors?
- Why should anyone invest in it? (credibility factors: track record, management team's expertise etc).
- How much finance is required, nature of funding (loans, grants, equity participation)?

Management team expertise
- Experience, qualifications, specialist knowledge of each of the founding members. Summarise to meet the requirements of your particular venture.

The concept
- Just what is your idea?
- Explain it fully but briefly.
- If it's brand new, prove its practicality.
- If it's been around for years, who else is doing it?
- What's different about your idea?
- Is there a gap in the market for it?

Methodology
- Describe on just one page exactly how your idea works in practice, step by step.
- Use a simple schematic to illustrate this.

Objectives
- List your objectives for the enterprise: personal and business, long and short term.
- Now show how you intend to realise these objectives.

Market
- Even though you think you know your market inside out, research it again fully before committing this section to paper.
- Describe the market, its characteristics and current trends.
- Show precisely where your product or service fits in.
- If it slots into a particular niche, describe this sub-sector.

Competition
- List the main competitors in your immediate catchment area.
- Detail their product ranges and illustrate where they differ from yours. If they are superior, say so; if they're not, explain why not.
- Give a breakdown of current competitive market shares.
- If you perceive a gap in the market for your particular product or service, guesstimate how you think the competition will react on your entry into the market.

The product
Some schools of thought have this section appearing before 'Market' and 'Competition' but I think it's best unveiled after you've talked about these aspects.
- Devote just one concise page to its description.
- If it's different from competitive alternatives, say so.
- If it's superior, say so.
- If it's inferior, say so and then explain why you believe there's

still a market for it.
- List the benefits to the end consumer.

Packaging the proposition
- Wrap concept, methodology and product into the benefits package you'll be offering your customers.
- One slight difference makes all the difference.
- Will it be discounting?
- Will it be incentive marketing?
- Will it be added value service?

Marketing your business
- Keep your marketing simple and relevant to your product or service.
- Avoid a convoluted approach.
- You should be planning a launch brochure.
- Think carefully before allocating monies for advertising.
- Plan for cost-free PR exposure.

Evolving the sales policy
- Your marketing strategy will determine the sales policy.
- Will you require a sales force?
- Will you engage the services of a major wholesaler?
- Will you be selling off-the-page?
- Will you sell by direct mail?

Units forecast
- If you're manufacturing, this is essential.
- Even if you're not, you'll still want to record the assignments or projects you are forecasting to complete.

Production costs
- Whether manufacturing or supplying a service, you'll be incurring production costs.
- Record your monthly forecasts.
- Will you be buying from only the one source?
- Will you be using several suppliers?
- Do you anticipate special terms with some of these suppliers?
- Make sure you record everything before you get to the bottom line.

Strengths and weaknesses
- Elaborate on the strengths of your scheme.
- No matter how brilliant, there are some weaknesses. Jot them down faithfully before someone else does it for you.

The case for public sector assistance
- If you feel you may have a case, here's the place to state it.
- Will you be employing local labour?
- Would you employ and train unemployed people?
- Is your business manufacturing based?
- Would you be interested in a local authority nest unit?
- Will you be trading outwith the local economy? (if you can answer yes to these questions, you'll be in line for public sector assistance).

Financial projections
Be precise in both your forecasting and your funding requirements:
- Profit & loss over 2/3 years.
- Cash flow over 2/3 years.
- Balance sheet for years 1, 2 (and 3).
- Start-up funding requirement.

You'll need some help with this. Make sure you ask for it.

Appendix
- CVs for yourself and your partner.
- Orders or written 'promises'.
- Anything else of relevance that doesn't fit in elsewhere.

CASE STUDIES

Tom's plan takes shape
Tom's days were no longer empty and depressing. In fact, some days he found himself working longer hours than when he was in a job and enjoying himself into the bargain. He'd borrowed some books on business administration from the public library and was making notes from the sections relevant to launching his own particular enterprise.

The initial sessions on team building and planning which Tom attended at his entrepreneurship programme were also proving to be both interesting and useful. Although he hadn't started to write it yet, his business plan was already beginning to take shape in his mind.

What excited Tom more than anything else was the fact that the skills he had acquired working for wages in the printing trade over 30 years were now being employed fashioning a venture of his very own. What's more, he could see that he could make money out of it – much more money than he'd ever made before.

Hazel and Paul disagree

'So, what do you think?' asked Hazel.

'Just a minute.' Paul was on the final page of the business plan Hazel had prepared for their mobile fast food venture. It contained twelve pages in all. It covered matters such as concept, trading name, the partners' respective qualifications and experience, territory of operation, start-up costs, profit margins, turnover and cash flow projections. 'Great, when do we start?'

'Not before we've laid our hands on £2,500,' replied Hazel.

'That's the bit I don't agree with. We don't need as much as another £2,500 to get us going. We could buy an old banger and a secondhand microwave and save a packet.'

'No. That wouldn't be saving, it would be wasting money. What if they both keep breaking down? We'd be out of business in no time.'

'No we wouldn't, I can fix things as good as anyone. You know I can.'

'Sure, but we need to keep your time for making up those lovely sandwiches and pastas. We can't have you working as a mechanic as well.'

'Point taken. You're the boss.'

'No I'm not, we're partners. Wait a minute though. Someone has to be in charge...'

'Like I said, you're the boss. Shall I call you Sir?...'

John and Colin visit the Enterprise Trust

'So, gentlemen, tell me what you have in mind.'

John and Colin were in the offices of the Enterprise Trust and had just been introduced to one of the Business Development Executives. John explained the bones of their idea and the outcome of the meeting with the Social Services. Colin had prepared a rough business plan. He passed around copies and gave the executive a run through on the salient points.

There would appear to be several chances of help: 'booster' grant, soft loan, and places on a refresher course on business administration for John and Colin. Another meeting was arranged for a few weeks hence when the executive would report back on progress.

EXERCISES

1. Visit your local public library and bookshops. Browse through the shelves for books on business administration and in particular, business planning. Choose the one(s) best suited to your particular needs.

2. Visit your local bank branches and obtain copies of their respective business start-up packs.

3. Make a start on assembling the bones of your plan, using the guidelines provided in this chapter.

4. Having completed (3) draft an executive summary to put at the front of your eventual business plan.

5. Make out an initial case for public sector assistance.

4

Funding Your Enterprise

GETTING YOUR HANDS ON SOME SEED MONEY

You'll need seed money to begin with and then, later, working capital to get your enterprise up and running.

Example: Focus Publishing International

I wish I could tell you that I found this easy. But I didn't. The only income I had at the time was from Social Security and the only spare cash I had left was barely enough for basic living expenses. The situation was dire for someone hell-bent on launching a business in six months' time. Even worse, the targeted launch date coincided with the time I reckoned I had to start earning or risk going under personally.

To attract sufficient working capital from an amalgam of commercial and public sector funding sources, I needed to raise a minimum of £10,000 as seed money or founder's equity, whatever you'd like to call it. (My partner had a similar brief.)

Show time: I did some serious soul searching, a little lateral thinking and a lot of praying. The £10,000 cash I needed urgently and didn't have. I had a house with just enough spare equity to cover the requirement but this was the final bastion – and anyway, how could I possibly demonstrate ability to repay? Did I have any friends or relations who might help out? I did but this was a route I didn't want to take. Some people don't mind accepting this kind of assistance. I do.

What else did I have? – two annuities on which I had somehow managed to keep up the contributions through thick and thin. They were only two years away from maturity and intended as a substitute for a pension (some pension). I decided to cash them in and lose a small fortune in the process. Then I thought again.

Magic, lateral thinking or inspiration

What if I could borrow £10,000 against the final maturity values but *defer* repayments until the due materialisation dates (which were within days of each other)? If this were possible then all I had to do was keep up the premiums which I had been doing anyway for eight years and clear off the respective loans in one go when both policies matured.

My initial approaches to the sources concerned were bounced out of court but with persistence, obduracy and persuasion I managed to convince them eventually that I was a good bet for such a deal.

My policies had been performing better than I realised and the loan cheques I received totalled £12,500, leaving me a comfortable balance to add to my budget for living expenses.

There's always a way

Chances are you're not as hard-pressed as I was then but if you are, take heart. There's *always* a way if you're determined enough to think it through to actuality.

So what are the limited key options available to you for raising some seed capital for your enterprise?

- personal resources
- insurance policies
- annuities
- spare equity on your home
- friends and relations
- bank loan (but you can't go back for more and your chances of getting an overdraft when you most need it are negligible).

Not a lot up for grabs, is there? But there's enough. If you really want it badly enough, want to strike out on your own, you'll find a way.

GETTING OUTSIDE FINANCE

Whatever the nature of your idea you'll almost certainly require additional investment from external sources to transform it into a reality.

Where do I start looking?

There are only two acceptable, safe options: private institutional and public sector sources. What you should aim for is an amalgam of both but with the emphasis on public sector assistance. We'll look at this in more detail a little later.

Who do I talk to in the private sector?

This will depend very much on the intended scale of your operation. If you're thinking small to begin with, then the best place to start is your bank manager but do not expect too much enthusiasm or understanding from that quarter. All banks have had their fingers burned in commercial lending over recent years and they tend to be scathing about approaches centred on start-up projects. Not very encouraging is it? Don't despair, though. We'll leave your bank manager to the very end.

On the other hand, if your idea is on the grand scale you ought to be having early conversations with venture capital houses and circulating your business plan around such as 3i, Charterhouse, Morgan Grenfell and the like. But these institutions will only take you seriously if your investment requirement has a minimum base of £500,000. If you're thinking big, talk to them.

APPROACHING THE PUBLIC SECTOR

A great deal is available from the public sector if you go about it the right way. This is the area you should concentrate on first. Why? – because you'll get a friendly ear to your initial overtures and an honest appraisal of your project.

So what is available?

Grants are great

The great thing about grants is that you don't have to pay them back. They come in all shapes and sizes: employment, training, marketing are among the ones most readily available for start-up projects. Don't be shy about asking. A roll-up package of these three grants can be very useful in your early trading days. In certain areas you will qualify for a New Business Grant for yourself if you are unemployed as I was. Employing others who are on the dole equally qualifies your enterprise for grants ranging up to 60 per cent of wages and National Insurance contributions for the first 26 weeks. Assistance with training is also available with grants up to 100 per cent for the first year. Marketing grants (available only in certain areas) range from 30 to 50 per cent.

Soft loans

Go for these first before you even discuss arranging a facility with your bank manager (I'll tell you why later). Now don't get too excited about the term 'soft'. There are no soft touches among the people you'll be dealing with and you'll have to pay back the money sometime. These loans are 'soft' only inasmuch as they are structured on very competitive terms, unsecured up to £10,000 and usually carry a capital repayment holiday of three to six months.

If you can satisfy the funders' criteria (which are not punitive) try to achieve much of the finance you will need from this area.

Free initial training for yourself

Even if you already consider yourself well versed in information technology, don't fail to take advantage of one of the various public sector sponsored technology training courses available to approved start-ups in many regions of the UK. The one my company opted for wasn't entirely free but for an investment of just £500 we got £1,500 worth of training plus brand new computer hardware and software with a combined price tag of £2,000. Getting our hands on £500 in the early days of trading wasn't easy but the effort expended paid off handsomely.

Where do you go for all these goodies?

What's specifically on offer very much depends upon where you intend to locate your enterprise but here is a general guide to availability which is by no means exhaustive. Look around for yourself in your own area and you'll find many more.

Grants

Department of Trade & Industry
Regional Enterprise
Regional Investment
Innovation
Research Support

Local Authority: Regional, County, District, Borough etc.
Various grants on offer. If your area is covered by two authorities, ie County Council and District Council, then approach both. You may well end up with several offers of grant assistance.

TEC (Training & Enterprise Council)
LEC (Local Enterprise Agency)
Employment
Training
Marketing

Local Enterprise Trusts
Start-up Booster Grants

Soft loans

Local Authority
Unsecured up to £5,000 in certain areas.

TECs/LECs
Unsecured up to £10,000.
Secured up to £50,000 and beyond.
Some will also consider equity participation.

Local Enterprise Trusts
Unsecured up to £5,000.

British Steel (Industry)
Available only in selected regions to assist in job creation.
Unsecured up to £25,000.
Larger Secured Loans also available.

British Coal (Enterprise)
Available only in selected regions to assist in job creation.
Unsecured up to £5,000.
Larger Secured Loans also negotiable.

Summary
Source first for funding through these public sector outlets. They're much more friendly and understanding and their loan terms are very competitive.

Now let's look at how you approach the funders, both private and public, and in what order.

APPROACHING POTENTIAL FUNDERS

Clearly, you won't even consider approaching any funder until you're 100 per cent happy about your business plan. You will need to feel confident that you will be able to field any questions that may arise during initial discussions – and arise they certainly will.

Let's assume your venture will be on a small to medium scale, and that the financial section of your plan has clearly identified the working capital requirement for the first 12/18 months of trading. You ought also to have made a stab at how this funding would be best and most readily achieved.

Example 1
A snapshot for a total investment package of say, £100,000, could look something like this if you set out to raise it exclusively from commercial funding sources:

Requirement	£100,000
Financed by	
Founders equity/Loans	£ 50,000
Term loan/Overdraft facility	£ 50,000*
Total finance	£100,000

*Totally secured by collateral

Example 2
Take the same package but change the lens for the snapshot to include public sector assistance:

Requirement	£100,000
Financed by	
Founders equity/Loans	£ 25,000
Public sector grants	£ 20,000
Public sector unsecured loans	£ 40,000
Bank overdraft	£ 15,000
Total finance	£100,000

Which deal are you going for?

The ratios between the two equations say it all. Dealing in the commercial sector alone you'll be doing well to achieve 50/50. Mix in public sector assistance and you will have additional numbers to play around with.

Example 3
If you think this is all a bit far fetched, let me show you now what my partner and I achieved on a total investment of £70,000, starting with bus fare only in my pocket:

Requirement	£70,000
Finance obtained	
Personal equity	£10,400
Partner's equity	£ 9,600
Public sector grants	£21,000
Public sector unsecured loans	£25,000
Bank overdraft	£10,000
Total finance	£76,000

Yes, we ended up with £6,000 more than bargained for in public sector assistance but still had to arrange for a £10,000 bank facility for reasons which I'll explain shortly.

My personal equity stake in the company came by way of borrowing against annuities and no bank would grant us an overdraft without back-to-back collateral. I had no money left to spare and I didn't have any in the first place. Solution? I borrowed another £10,000 on a credit card (no questions asked) and stuck it in a high interest savings account as collateral against an overdraft we barely needed to draw on anyway.

What did I say? There's always a way.

Now that you know why we're going to leave the bank manager to the very end, let's establish the batting order in your approach for funding:

Public sector

But make no approach until you've studied everything on offer in your local area; made a value judgement on which grants would be applicable and whether you have sufficient grounds for qualifying; which and what levels of unsecured loan assistance your embryo business could afford in the very early days. Do your homework thoroughly. Leave nothing out of your 'needs' reckoning but ask for not a penny more than your plan calls for (despite my experience).

(a) Local Council Economic Development/Local Enterprise Trust
Better a tiny fish in a small pond to begin with. If your business proposition is sound, you'll be an important client with prospects of contributing to the local economy in tandem with your own growth. Should they offer to act as a catalyst on your behalf with agencies further up the pecking order (TECs, LECs) then grasp the opportunity with grateful hands. They will get you there quicker than you will be able to on your own. Their links with British Steel, British Coal and similar big institutions are also formidable.

(b) TECs/LECs
Go to these organisations first only if your enterprise calls for substantial external investment or if you have graduated from one of their **Entrepreneurship Programmes** (you'll have an edge if you have). Once again, if they offer to join in on discussions with venture capital houses, agree at once to their participation.

There's one near you:

- 82 TECs throughout England and Wales.

- 22 LECS throughout Scotland.

Complete listings for all of these are shown in the Appendix.

(c) British Steel (Industry)/British Coal (Enterprise)
These organisations are best approached with Local Authority endorsement of your business plan and preferably in the company of their representatives.

Commercial sources
If your venture is small to medium, this means the bank. Go here last and only when you've got the rest of your funding in position, *ie* your own investment, your partner's investment and public sector grants and loans. Banks only lend to start-ups on totally secured, belt and braces conditions. You've got to get one of them interested but take only as little as you need.

THE PLAN THAT WILL FIX YOUR FUNDING

Follow these suggestions to the letter. They're based on my personal experience. They worked for me and they'll work for you.

Step 1

Expect and allow for many meetings with your chosen public sector funders. Patience is the name of the game. The initial enthusiasm of their new business teams will be quickly replaced by seemingly sanguine indifference from the investment managers. Don't be put off. On the contrary, take careful heed of any suggestions they put forward about your overall plan. It's all part of the game. They know better than you the route to successfully enacting your grant and loan applications. Listen to them and they'll help you, although you may not think so at the time.

Step 2

Accept from the outset that it's all a bit of a game and there's a hidden agenda that no one's going to tell you about (except me). Don't worry, the pieces will all eventually fall neatly into place as long as you are totally honest in all your conversations with the public authority people. But here's a really key tip.

- *You will require to convince all of them individually and collectively that your plan is sound and worthy of public sector assistance.*

That's a tall order considering that it's well nigh impossible to get them all together at the same time for a corporate meeting on your proposition.

Here's what you do to convince them all individually and collectively without getting them all together face to face.

(a) You're confident about your new venture. Now prove that you have reason to be confident. Go out and get some orders confirmed in writing (or if you can't manage that yet, some promises). Circulate the news to all concerned by fax.

(b) Zero in on the one funder with whom you feel most comfortable. This will almost certainly be the one who'll get the brownie points when you get your funding. Make this person your first point of call. Keep up the pressure until you get a letter confirming a deal. You'll get that letter.

(c) Send faxes to the others advising them of the funding break-through.

Get one to say 'Yes' and the others will fall into line rapidly.

Step 3

Now you can go to the bank manager. In fact you'll have to go to the bank manager because the offers of grant aid and loan assistance you have received from the public sector will be conditional on your ability to raise the balance of your funding from the *commercial* sector by whatever means you can. It's no good suddenly finding this balance from your hip pocket or producing a bundle of cash from a friendly aunt. Those are the rules and there are no exceptions.

But now you know something no one else is going to tell you, so you can go funds-sourcing with a degree of confidence.

The 'Fax that'll Fix the Funding'

Use and adapt this example to secure your funding.

To: Ralph Graves, Anywhere Training & Enterprise Council

From: Ed Wynn, Sensor Batteries

Subject: Grant & Loan Applications

New Business Gains

Yesterday afternoon I completed negotiations on two very important pieces of new business representing a combined contribution of £45,000 to the first month's trading performance of Sensor Batteries. As work begins immediately on both of these assignments, I am sure you will appreciate the urgency of an early and favourable decision on my company's Grant & Loan Applications.

The good news doesn't stop here...

I have several other tenders moving along rapidly to maturity and expect to be able to report back shortly with news of further acquisitions.

Regards

ED WYNN

PRESENTING YOUR CASE

Wrapping up the package

How you present yourself and your case for assistance is key to obtaining early and favourable decisions all round. How you finally wrap your package and present it to the decision-makers is equally vital.

There was a time not too long ago when you only heard of advertising agents making presentations. Now, it seems, everyone's doing it. But you can learn a lot from the way ad agents go about it. Their presentations are very professional, very fast and get to the heart of the matter with a touch of style. They are also very expensive.

Five tricks of the trade

Now, I'm not suggesting you invest a bundle of money in your presentation but there are some tricks of the trade worth embracing:

1. Make sure that the final version of your business plan is professionally executed, is free of errors (literal and numerical), has a distinctive cover and is securely bound. If you don't have access to a word processing facility, rent one.

2. Have copies of your proposal in the hands of all the participants at least two weeks prior to each meeting.

3. If you are unused to presenting to others, practise beforehand on family or friends. Don't waste time feeling awkward about it. Ask them to be objective in their appraisal of your performance.

4. Speak up when you get there. It's your show. You're on and you're centre stage. Don't leave it to the others to open the dialogue or cover up awkward gaps in the conversation later on.

5. Above all: keep on the lookout for buying signals and when you receive an offer which is favourable to you, *Shut Up*, pack up and go away. Don't even wait for a cup of coffee or you may find yourself going suicidal and talking your way out of the deal you've worked so hard to put together. It happens.

CHECKLIST

- Describe how you will obtain seed money to get you started.

- List various sources you could approach to raise seed capital.

- Look at ways you might attract external funding.

- Name potential supply sources in the private sector.

- Make out a case for public sector assistance.

- Describe what is readily available from the public sector.

- Highlight the core advantage in grant funding.

- Describe 'soft loans'.

- Locate free training opportunities for skills improvement.

- List all the sources for public sector assistance.

- Explain why you would contact the public sector first.

- Explain why you would leave the banks until last.

- How would you present your case for assistance?

- Why is it important to package it properly?

CASE STUDIES

Tom seeks an experienced partner

Tom's initial plan was to go it alone in his new enterprise. However, he was some weeks now into his entrepreneurial programme and already discovering several good reasons why it was necessary to be taking seriously the matter of looking around for a partner.

To begin with, maths was never Tom's strong point. He was going to need some professional help when he got around to preparing financial forecasts for his business plan. Moreover, once the business was up and running, who would look after the bookkeeping and administration? His wife didn't seem too keen (anyway she was in regular employment).

It had also occurred to Tom that his own initial cash injection for the business might not be enough to attract external funding. What he needed was an equity partner with specialist skills in management accounting and administration – and some capital to invest in the enterprise.

He decided to start looking for one.

A guarantor for Paul and Hazel

Paul and Hazel had their first meeting with the Business Development department of the county's Training & Enterprise Council. The department couldn't offer direct assistance but commended their initiative and made an appointment for them to visit a government agency specialising in youth incentive schemes. Our entrepreneurs met again later in the day.

'Guess what? I showed dad our plan and told him about the meeting with the TEC, and guess what?'

'What?'

'He's offered to go guarantor for a £1,000 bank loan! We've got an appointment with the bank manager for tomorrow afternoon.'

'That's great news. Aren't dads just wonderful? He must own that dustcart...'

Colin and John agree their finances

Colin had by now made good progress on refining the business plan for 'Comely Coaches', the name under which they agreed the partnership would trade. John had located a nearly-new 12 seater minibus which was well within budget, and costed out several other essential pieces of equipment. They had also agreed the capital to be introduced into the business by each of them. It was to be a 50-50 split.

All in all Colin and John were well fixed for the next meeting with the Enterprise Trust which was just a few days away.

ACTION POINTS

Tackle each of the following points according to whether you already have a business idea or whether you're still thinking about it (in which case use a hypothetical scenario).

1. Make out an itemised list of your initial seed capital requirement

and then determine how you will go about fulfilling the requirement.

2. What private and commercial sources could be available to you for external investment in your enterprise? Draw up a list.

3. Which public sector sources within your area could you approach for financial assistance by way of soft loans and grants? Draw up a list.

4. Evaluate your total funding requirement by (a) commercial investment only and (b) a mix of commercial and public sector funding.

5. Write the copy for your own personal 'fax that'll fix the funding' (see page 52).

6. Draft two brief presentation scripts intended for (a) commercial funders and (b) public sector funding sources.

5

Planning Ahead

Before you launch your new business you'll want to be planning ahead for every eventuality. It may be you'll need a partner to make it work; now's the time to be thinking about this. You'll certainly want to measure up the competition and you'll need to think about premises and systems.

CHOOSING A PARTNER

If (like me) you're a loner by nature, you may be wondering why I include choosing a partner as a vital step in starting up. I include it for one reason and one reason only. If your new venture calls for outside capitalisation, you won't get it unless you can show clear evidence of team building in your plans. Lending sources in both the private and public sectors are mustard on this condition nowadays. A friend or relation prepared to invest some money in your idea is helpful but not nearly enough. You still won't get the cash unless your prospectus includes a strong section on management expertise. This does not mean to say you have to join up with several partners. Just one will do as long as he or she has specialist skills that complement your own. Who knows, a member of your family might fit the bill.

Finding the right partner
Your best bet is to sign up for one of the Entrepreneurship Programmes mentioned in an earlier chapter (page 23). I joined my course with that as a prime aim and I was successful in achieving it. But it didn't just happen; I had to work at it. The programme gave me a platform from which I could view and assess the various alternatives. That, as I perceived it, was the core benefit in joining. I was going ahead anyway with my plan for a new business, but I knew that to attract the necessary external finance, I also had to attract a suitable equity participating partner. These programmes are composed of an

enviable mix of skills and experience. Whatever you're looking for is almost certainly bound to be available if you can just get the chemistry right.

The qualities to look for in a partner

There are five specific areas you'll want to investigate thoroughly when considering who is going to run with you in your new enterprise.

Integrity

Very difficult to assess in advance but make every effort to do so. He/she is hopefully going to be around for a long time to come, so be absolutely certain the successful candidate has lots and lots of this essential quality.

Complementary skills

For example, if you are the one who's going to be flying the nest every morning looking for business, you'll want to have someone reliable back at the office doing the books, conceiving and implementing systems and generally attending to all other matters of administration.

Experience

Establish right from the outset that your selected partner has a quantifiable track record in performing all the skills you need but don't have personally. Academic qualifications are fine up to a point but nothing really equals practical experience.

Solvency

If you are to attract the external finance you've identified as critical to your new business, your chances of success will be much greater if your partner is also investing in the seed funding. However, what some people say they will do and what they will actually do on the due date can vary dramatically. Make quite sure of the candidate's solvency and net worth before committing yourself to any deal. Don't be afraid to ask. It's your own future you'll be risking if you don't.

Choosing a partner: points to consider

1. Make out a list of the ideal qualities you would be looking for in a potential partner to join you in your new enterprise. Add to the list outlined in this chapter.

2. Think of six different ways you could go about finding a suitable partner.

3. Having evaluated your own commercial skills what complementary skills would you require in the chosen candidate?

4. Is there a family member, friend or colleague who might be worthy of serious consideration?

CASE STUDIES: GOING INTO PARTNERSHIP

Tom looks around for assistance

Tom had now completed the first rough draft of his business plan. It was evident that for his new venture to be on steady ground from day one, he had insufficient cash available for seed capital. Tom was using what was left of his savings and redundancy payment but both had been seriously depleted during his months of unemployment.

Tom had also completed his initial sourcing for an equity partner. It hadn't proved too difficult after all; on the entrepreneurship programme were several management accountants (some still employed, some not) and he'd struck up an acquaintance with each of them. Following deliberation he made his mind up to approach the one who best met the qualities he would be requiring in a financially participating soul mate.

He outlined his proposal to his colleague, handed over a copy of the plan and asked for a reaction within a week. Seven days later Tom had found his business partner, Paula (33) an unemployed management accountant. Paula now went to work on Tom's roughly hewn financial calculations to get them into shape.

Hazel's bank guarantee

The meeting with the bank manager went well (as well it might with Hazel's dad putting up the collateral for the loan) and immediately afterwards our intrepid entrepreneurs visited the offices of the Youth Incentive Scheme (entitled in their area 'The Junior Partnership') for a discussion on how best they might obtain the balance of their funding.

'As you can see from the business plan,' said Hazel to the new business executive, 'we need £3,000 in total to get us up and running. My dad's already given us £500 as seed money, we've got a loan of £1,000 from the bank which dad again is guaranteeing, so we're shy of £1,500. Can you help us?'

Following an hour's discussion it was agreed that an application should be made for a New Business Grant (which is a replacement for the old Enterprise Allowance Scheme). This would qualify each of them for a weekly payment for the first year of trading. The executive would also look into the possibility of another grant or soft loan or both to make up the balance.

John and Colin get the good news and the bad news
Back again at the Local Enterprise Trust with their updated plan and costings, John and Colin discussed the possibility of financial assistance from the public sector for their project.

The Business Development Executive explained that he had good news and some bad news for them. The bad news was that because 'Comely Coaches' was a project solely devoted to community service and unlikely to have employment growth potential, the best on offer was therefore a grant of £1,000 from the European Social Fund. Neither John or Colin regarded that news as a body blow.

The good news was that the executive had discussed their plan with a local philanthropist who liked what he heard and had requested an early meeting with both of them.

It was confirmed that both John and Colin had been accepted for the Business Administration Refresher Course, the expense of which would be paid by the Enterprise Trust. Not a bad day's work, after all.

MEASURING THE COMPETITION

However innovative the idea upon which your new business plan is based, someone else has thought of it before you.

Learning to live with competition
You could have invented a cordless toaster that runs on fresh air, butters and marmalades its produce and then sweeps up the crumbs. Someone's bound to be marketing something similar just around the corner. But don't let that put you off. Competition is the spice of business life. In fact, without it there would be very little creative activity in your marketplace.

Finding out as much as you can
Right from the start it will pay you to find out as much as you can

about the people with whom you'll be jousting for orders. How do you go about this intelligence gathering? Easy. Many of your competitors are unable to contain themselves every time they're on a roll, they will employ expensive PR consultants to broadcast the news in the journals of your trade. We are not necessarily talking about large conglomerates who can afford this sort of indulgence. Many small concerns who can't afford it also employ public relations specialists. So, right from day one, subscribe to the key trade papers and start a cuttings service of your own. Don't pay anyone else to do this for you. Do it yourself, it's an excellent discipline.

Asking the clientele

Another good and reliable way of keeping up to date with competitive activity is to ask your customers. They won't mind. If they're getting good service, they'll tell you. If not, they'll also tell you, and there is your opportunity.

What sort of activity should you be monitoring in particular?

Checking your competitor ranges

Look early and carefully at the range of products/services marketed by each of your competitors. Do they vary much from yours? If so, how much and in what ways? Be honest and detailed in your appraisal. Are they better than you at some things? Would it pay you to adjust your range and come into line with the best on offer from the competition?

Checking operational areas

Dig deeply and establish who's doing what on your patch. It's not necessarily the biggest who gets the lion's share. Concentrate on the activities of the local market leader in your field and try to find out what makes them tick. Have they been around a long time? Is it their pricing policy, their marketing? Or do the rest of the competition think they've got it sewn up and just leave them to it? (There might be an opening here.)

Deciding your prices

This is always rather a problem when you're starting out. The temptation can be strong to start with suicidally low margins or to take on assignments on a fee-based structure that you haven't a hope in hell of making any money out of. Try hard to avoid this route. You may have to turn down some business in the process but you must start the way you mean to go on: giving good service for a fair return. Don't be rushed into giving it all away just to get a few orders. Be patient.

Monitor your competition rigorously on their pricing policies. They've been at it longer than you, they've made their mistakes and learned from them. When you're tempted to undercut, think long and hard before you do. You may have to live with the painful effects of your impetuosity for a very long time.

Distribution channels
This may or may not be an issue depending upon the nature of your enterprise. If it is, study the distribution patterns of the competition before committing finally to the methods you will use. It could be very expensive if you don't get things synchronised from the beginning.

Establishing market shares
You might find this information easy to come by. I didn't. The industry I operate in is very much of a 'closed' nature (though I did manage eventually to acquire what I needed). Whatever, you need to find out, but remember it's only your immediate catchment area you're bothered about. You'll find a way.

Promotional activity
- Does your competition advertise heavily?
- Which media do they use?
- Do they exhibit at trade or consumer shows?
- Do they run incentive schemes for the trade?
- Do they operate premium offers for end users?
- How much do they budget for promotion?

You'll need reliable information on all these activities before you plan your own albeit limited programme.

Strengths/weaknesses of the competition
No matter how you may perceive your competition initially – or indeed how they perceive themselves – there will be well defined strengths and weaknesses in their structure which you must become acquainted with. You may not discover this intelligence for some time, and not at all without a lot of delving and observation. But when you do, it will be of immense value to your embryonic venture. Emulate their strengths, and try to capitalise on and learn from their weaknesses.

Putting your knowledge of the competition to work

When you've gathered together all this accumulated intelligence, put it to work on your behalf. Study the findings carefully. Pick out the core elements and concentrate on them as you start to prepare your own initial strategic marketing plan. This way you will learn to discipline yourself always to be aware of the competition and their marketing activity.

Questionnaire: how ready are you to face the competition?

- How much do you know about the competition
  for your idea?   _____

- How much can you find out?   _____

- Where's the best place to start asking?   _____

- What knowledge do you have of the ranges the
  competition offer?   _____

- What are their areas of operation?   _____

- Do you know their pricing policies?   _____

- Do you know the market shares?   _____

- What sort of promotional activities does the
  the competition undertake?   _____

- What are their strengths and weaknesses?   _____

- How would you put your accumulated knowledge
  to work?   _____

FINDING THE RIGHT PREMISES

You will have already given serious consideration to premises in putting together your business plan and initial budget. You may have decided, as I did, to operate your venture out of a room in your own home (or your partner's) for the first few months of trading. There's nothing wrong with that. It conserves cash and is quite acceptable nowadays to most funders. You obviously can't go on that way for ever, but it will allow you some valuable breathing space before making what may well be the single biggest decision you will face in expenditure and commitment in your new enterprise.

There's another way to begin operations before committing to a lease and I recommend you give it serious consideration.

Getting help from the public sector

The Business Centres which house Local Enterprise Trusts frequently offer start-ups a flexible deal. Typically, you can opt for renting accommodation and secretarial services on a short term basis or, if you prefer, an accommodation facility for mail, messages and secretarial help. Their terms are very reasonable and you can cancel the arrangement anytime it suits you without incurring a penalty.

Before you sign on the dotted line

Make the Local Enterprise Trust your first port of call when you start to look seriously for permanent premises. The Trust will know what's available locally and what will best suit your needs. They are in daily contact with both the commercial and public sector property agents in your area. Talk to them, listen to them and take their advice before you sign on the dotted line. Watch out for business rates.

THE SYSTEMS YOU WILL NEED

Personal organisation

The best place to start is yourself. If *you're* organised it's a lot easier to organise everyone else around you. The essential tools you'll need won't cost much: an A4 pad and a pen. Last thing every night before you retire, list all the things you have to do the next day, then put them in order of priority with the nastiest piece of business right up there at the top. Crack that one first in the morning and the rest will disappear off your list in no time.

Treat every day in your new venture as an *ad*venture. To do that effectively, you must be personally very well organised.

Relevant and complementary systems

You'll need to devise and operate systems which complement your particular enterprise. There's nothing difficult about this but don't overdo the systems. Keep them relevant and simple. Whatever else, do concentrate on developing a system for effective debt collection suited to the nature of your business.

Using the help available

Browse through the business section of any major bookseller and you'll find a plethora of excellent and inexpensive paperbacks with tailormade systems and forms to cover the needs of almost any enterprise: accounting, distribution, sales, wages, tax, VAT etc. Select the one that best suits your needs and adapt it accordingly.

Any other specific systems you may require will come to light along the way and you can devise them for yourself.

DECIDING YOUR BUSINESS STATUS

You have a choice of three possible routes with regard to the status of your enterprise. Your eventual choice will largely depend on the nature of the business.

Becoming a sole trader
There are certain initial financial advantages in operating as a sole trader but I would caution against it if you are looking for more substantial outside investment. Funders aren't too enthusiastic about lending to a one man or woman operation. Taxwise it is great for the first two years – but beware the new tax regulations for the self-employed.

The big disadvantage of the sole trader operation is that (God forbid) should it go down the pan you will be liable for all debts personally – unlimited liability, in fact.

Forming a partnership
In a partnership you and your partner legally share everything, the good and the bad. Your shares can be 50-50 or any other split you agree upon but always remember that once again you are faced with unlimited liability and you will each be responsible (separately and jointly) for all liabilities incurred in the name of the partnership.

Partnerships are obligatory in certain professional spheres, so again the nature of the business will determine whether this is the route to take. Otherwise do give it great consideration before deciding.

I would personally never enter into a partnership in business. Most partnership agreements are far too loosely defined and fraught with legal and financial hazards. Try getting out of one with your shirt intact when all goes wrong. To say it's not easy is an understatement.

Forming a limited company
This status will give you the most protection in all eventualities. Provided you act honestly and correctly, your personal liability is limited to the share capital you have invested in the company.

Paradoxically you are likely to receive a friendlier ear when you go asking for external funding. But don't be fooled. You still have to give the banks belt-and-braces security against anything you borrow. Typically this will include having to give your personal guarantee for the company's overdraft or bank loans, and pledging personal assets such as a house in support of such guarantee.

As a limited company you'll also have a lot more clout with the public sector in the matter of grant and loan funding.

Think about it. Then ask your solicitor and accountant for professional advice.

UNDERSTANDING THE BASICS OF TAXATION

No matter how fulfilling you find running your own business, no matter how much money you make, you'll be simply chasing your tail and heading for trouble if you don't turn your attention to the basics of the taxation process:

- Income tax
- National Insurance contributions (NICs)
- Value Added Tax (VAT).

Who do you need to tell you've started a business?
As soon as you start up in business you must inform:

- your local tax office
- the Contributions Agency
- Customs & Excise (if your taxable turnover is to be in excess of £48,000 per annum, you must register for VAT)
- your Job Centre (if you are registered with one).

What is income tax?
The main tax most people require to pay is income tax, which is charged on earnings of all kinds as well as on investment income such as bank interest. When you become self-employed or start up on your own in business you become responsible for paying your own tax and that is why you need to keep full and accurate records of all your business transactions.

Preparing your accounts
If you employ the services of an accountant, he will draw up your

accounts. But whoever prepares them, you are still responsible for their accuracy and the correct declaration of the amount of profits.

Under Self Assessment, you do *not* require to send in your accounts with your tax return. Instead you will be requested to include the accounts information in a special section of the return. Your tax office may ask to see your accounts together with your business records to check against the figures in your completed return.

Simple tax returns
If your business turnover (total sales) before expenses is below £15,000 for a full year of trading, you will not have to provide detailed accounts information in the return. Instead, a simple three line summary will suffice. For example:

Turnover	£13,847
Less purchases and expenses	£ 3,017
Net profits	£10,830

Taxation for partnerships

Special rules apply for income tax purposes if you are in business with a partner. Basically your tax bill is calculated as if *your share* of the partnership is profits that you have made in business on your own.

What does 'Self Assessment' mean?

The new Self Assessment system is intended to make individual tax matters clearer to people who regularly get tax returns. It is not a new tax.

What are National Insurance contributions?

These are five classes of contributions and the class you pay depends on whether you are an employee, self-employed, non-employed or an employer.

Self-employed persons are liable to pay two classes of contributions:

- Class 2 contributions

and

- Class 4 contributions, which are paid on profits and gains at or above a set level.

What is VAT?

VAT stands for 'Value Added Tax' and is a tax levied on most goods and services by the suppliers of those goods and services. Almost any business transaction can constitute what is known as a 'taxable supply' for VAT purposes, for example:

- sale of goods

- performance of services

- an exchange of goods or services

- a gift in kind.

Taxable supplies can be chargeable to VAT at the following rates:

- Zero rate: nil percentage applies

- Reduced rate: 8 per cent (limited to domestic fuel and power)

- Standard rate: 17.5 per cent (applied to all goods and services not exempt or liable at zero or reduced rates).

PREPARING TO SURVIVE – AND SUCCEED

Creating the right image

It's really important that you get this building block right, right from the start – so important that Chapter 6 examines the matter in detail. Remember, the image you will be creating for your business will be very largely influenced by the personal image you portray to the many and diverse personalities you will encounter in your day-to-day activities. Start working on a good personal image now. Get it right and you won't have to tinker with it later.

Surviving as a beginner

We are all beginners at the outset of any new enterprise. Indeed, this is no bad thing. Try hard not to surround yourself with 'experts' in your particular calling. Not only do they cost a lot of money, they are all too often set in their ways and unwilling to learn anything new. I've always gone for brightness and enthusiasm before experience in the many new ventures I've been involved in over the years and never had cause to regret it.

Marketing your enterprise

People launching out on their own for the first time are often uneasy about the mechanics of marketing. They express concern about finding the correct application for their particular enterprise. Worry not. Chapter 6 will tell you in plain English what 'marketing' is and what it is definitely not. There's no mystique about it, only common sense.

Developing a sales strategy
Once you've developed your initial marketing strategy, you will find that the sales strategy for your business falls neatly into place. Start thinking about it now. Chapters 6 and 7 will lead you gently through the process of research to marketing to selling. Don't rush to them now though; read through the book in its entirety once, then go back to 5, 6 and 7 and study them again.

CASE STUDIES

Tom and Paula reach some key decisions
Tom meanwhile was pleased with his choice of partner. Paula had made substantial progress on developing the business plan and already they were discussing external funding, premises, business systems and the legal status their joint enterprise was to take.

As they were now both committed to the business they held their first (unofficial) board meeting and made decisions on the following:

1. They would form a limited company.

2. Tom would have 60 per cent of the equity, Paula 40 per cent.

3. They would make early approaches to the public sector about possible grants and soft loan assistance.

4. They set a date three months hence for the launch of the enterprise.

5. Business would be initially conducted from Paula's home.

6. Tom would start sourcing equipment.

7. He would also start making appointments to visit his previous customers, advising them of the launch date.

   Tom's dream was beginning to turn into a reality.

A bonus for Paul and Hazel
'Hey, I've just found our gravy wagon and I can get it for £350 less than you've budgeted for.'

'Paul, we don't want an old banger. We agreed.'

'But it's not a banger, it's in great nick. It belongs to Mr Pearson who's been on the same fast food route for years. He's retiring and what's more, we get his route thrown in for free. He says he doesn't want a cowboy moving in.'

'Fantastic, Paul. Now we just need to hear from "The Junior Partnership" that our funding's okay and we're in business...'

John and Colin raise £5,000

John and Colin visited the local philanthropist at his home. Mr Watling had already studied the updated business plan which had been sent on to him in advance. He told them he was very interested in their project. He said he would like to invest some capital for which he did not require a return, only assurance that the money would be used solely as working capital. John and Colin received a cheque for £5,000.

ACTION POINTS

1. Draw up a brief outline of the accommodation you envisage your new enterprise will require for, say, an initial two year period. Will you really need premises for the first twelve months or so? Could you work from a room at home? Could you convert your garage?

2. Secondly, outline the basic systems you will need to begin with. Keep these systems simple and relevant and decide how best and cost-effectively you can implement them (purchasing, stock control, accounts, invoicing, cash collection, mailshots etc).

3. Look at the three options available to you in determining the legal status of your business. Which is best for you? What are the main implications of your final selection?

4. What kind of image do you want your business to reflect to others? Draw up an outline plan to achieve this.

5. What number and calibre of staff will you need at the outset? Work out job descriptions for each staff member.

6. Draw up a summary of your very first marketing strategy. From this plan devise the sales strategy for your business.

6

Marketing Your Enterprise

There is an incredible amount of rubbish talked about marketing. Much of it is based on little more than high-sounding jargon designed more to keep marketing pundits in business than to help business managers in the real world.

DEBUNKING THE MARKETING MYTH

Let's start with a basic definition of marketing:

- *Marketing is absolutely everything connected with the process by which a potential customer decides to buy (or not to buy).*

- Or, *marketing is communication.*

Communication is the essence of all business – and it's not necessarily the 'best talkers' who communicate best. You can communicate equally well by how you project your unique personality, how you articulate, how you relate to people without using words at all, how you listen to others.

What marketing is *not* is advertising, promotions, public relations, exhibitions, premiums, grand openings, closing down sales and the like – at least, not on their own individually or even collectively. It certainly includes all of these but a great deal more besides.

Marketing means a common sense approach to conducting your business. It starts and ends with *you*: how you dress, how you speak, how you approach your customers, how you treat your staff, how you set up your stall, in short, what kind of image you create for yourself and your enterprise.

It also has a lot to do with effective systems: how to react to problems, what kind of letters you send out, how to go about getting the cash in.

Let's examine a few of these essential aspects of pure marketing in the order of importance in which I would place them.

CREATING THE RIGHT PERSONAL IMAGE

Here's where your marketing programme really starts: with *you*. When you go out selling, you'll be marketing something much more potent than your product or service: you'll be selling *you* and you'll never stop selling *you*. Even when you've got a dozen salesmen out hustling, they'll still be selling *you*. This is not to imply that you ought to start thinking about changing *you*. You couldn't even if you tried. What it means is you have to be aware of *you* all the time and everywhere. How you project, how you dress, how you speak, how you earn (not command) respect. You're *you*. You're unique. Make the most of *you*. Think of some outstanding winners such as Richard Branson (Virgin), Anita Roddick (Bodyshop), or Victor Kiam (Remington).

The image your business will reflect
Customers, suppliers and staff will all develop an image of your new business in direct line with the image you project of yourself. They will see the business exactly according to the way you project it to them.

Millions of pounds are wasted annually by thousands of established companies in a vain attempt to improve their image. The problem frequently lies at the top, but has been around for so long that no one can see it for the fudge. That's how PR consultancies get rich. Make sure *you* get it right from the start.

Developing good customer relations
Clearly, if you don't get this right from the outset, you won't be around long enough to worry about the remainder of your marketing programme. But it's amazing how many start-ups make heavy weather of what is essentially a basic issue of dealing properly with other human beings – simple things, like correspondence, facing up to problems, cash collection, and the like. Every letter you send out should be an ambassador for your company: if you're unsure about the right style and format for a tricky situation, call on some help (there are several useful books on the market detailing suitable replies to almost every scenario you're likely to come across).

When faced with problems, address them immediately they come to light. You may not agree with the customer's point of view on all occasions but you must respect his right to express it. Try always to employ the 'win-win' formula, leaving the customer his dignity.

The right way to collect the cash
Getting the cash in on time is vital to every enterprise but most particularly so for the start-up. Never be afraid to ask for what you are due, when it is due. But do yourself a favour: be explicit from the start as to *exactly* what your payment terms are. Go on reminding your customers on every invoice and every statement you send out.

All the other good things you are doing will go for nought if you fail to get the cash in on time, every time. It's all to do with conditioning. To get your invoices nearer the top of the pile each month, condition your customers accordingly and keep on conditioning them. They won't tell you to shove off. They'll privately respect you for your principles (grudgingly perhaps, but that's okay).

Developing good staff relations
Even if your entire staff consists of just one other, there are two things you must accomplish without delay:

- Earn the respect of your staff through evidence of your own commitment.

- Instill in your staff your own personal philosophy of the business.

It sounds obvious, doesn't it? – so obvious in fact that most start-ups tend to ignore these two factors, imagining perhaps that respect should be automatic and that staff don't need to concern themselves with the philosophy behind the enterprise.

This is quite wrong. The best way to build your business in the early days is from within. Breed loyalty through involvement and you create a lasting team.

Now we can progress to what most people consider to be 'marketing' but believe me, unless you are prepared to develop the right personal and business image, customer and staff relations, what you are about to read isn't worth a light.

Managing your promotional activities
This will sound like heresy coming from someone who spent 30 years

at the top of the communications industry, but

- **Don't rush out and hire an advertising agency, a marketing specialist or a public relations consultancy.**

— Even if you reckon you need one of these, don't do it.
— Even if you've budgeted for it, don't do it.
— Even if the funders recommend it, don't do it.

Why not?

- **Because for the first 12 months you'll be far too busy developing your own personal image for *your* enterprise and the last thing you'll need is for some specialist who hasn't a clue about what makes you tick to create a false or artificial image for you which may turn out to be a Frankenstein monster that will devour you.**

If after a year you think the business warrants it, then go out and hire all three if you like, but not before.

So what sort of promotional activity are you going to undertake during your initial year of trading? In short, not a lot and only that which is absolutely necessary and which you can afford. By not a lot, I mean not a lot that costs you money but there's a great deal of useful work you can do for next to nothing.

Building up your image

This is the very first thing you give your attention to and here's where I advise you spend a *little* money to ensure that it's right, right from the start. We are all of us gifted with at least some personal creativity. When I reviewed a series of personally produced logos for my own company I thought one of them was absolutely brilliant. But when I took a step back, I began to realise that not only was it naff, it was also unworkable because of technical reproduction reasons (and the logo was produced by a trained designer).

Call in some objective, unbiased professional help: not a high priced design consultancy. There are lots of bright proficient young people out there with Apple Macs who will do you a superb job at the right price. Just explain in your own words what you're all about, and let them come up with proposals. Make sure, too, that you don't cheesepare on your stationery. Choose good quality paper and printing.

Get the 'front of the house' right too. Even if your reception area is the size of a broom closet, invest a little money to create an ambience where you can portray your business with a touch of class.

Creating your first brochure

You're going to require some modest piece of print matter to explain your enterprise and why prospective customers or clients should consider using you. Again this will cost a little money, but not too much if you go about its production in the right way.

First off, write down some notes about your initial customer base. Then go back and chat to your friendly young designer, and get him/her to produce a rough outline in tandem with the image already created. Ask him/her to call in a 'tame' printer (they will all know several who are as hungry as they are) and get a detailed written quote for printing the number you require. You won't be disappointed in the price.

There's something in it for both of them. It's called networking: the development of business through a growing network of contacts working with each other. Then, when your brochure has been produced (and if you've been successful in obtaining a marketing support grant) send a copy of it together with copies of all the relevant invoices to your local TEC/LEC and you could well get a rebate of 30 to 50 per cent. That's networking, too.

MARKETING RESEARCH

Here we will see how your business can be helped by 'marketing' research (as distinct from 'market' research). You'll want to be thinking about extending your limited promotional activity into other areas of your market. These areas are already well defined but you may have no idea how to approach them or whom to approach. This is a very common situation for start-up concerns and one best tackled as quickly as possible. It is also an area where you can do yourself a lot of good at minimal expense. Let's take for example the launch of my own enterprise.

Example
The business of my company is specialist publishing, exclusively for local authorities throughout the United Kingdom. The patch I really knew (including competitor activity) was Scotland and the North East of England. The remainder of the UK market was well defined through trade directories, but what I didn't know was which officer

had the responsibility for which of several relevant publications in which region, county, borough or district. Before pressing the print button on my company brochure I needed to establish actual *contact* points for the entire market. But how?

Easy! I went straight to the top. I penned a carefully worded letter accompanied by a simple questionnaire and prepaid reply envelope to every Chief Executive in every region, county, borough and district in the United Kingdom. The letter didn't mention it came from a business start-up but simply asked for help in updating current intelligence on publishing contact points within the local authority.

A dramatic response
The response factor was dramatic. Out of 800-odd requests, I received 523 impeccably completed responses. This yielded a potential customer database of 1,400 names to whom I mailed out personalised letters (plus brochure). From this exercise I derived excellent conversion ratios: over 100 qualified requests for appointments over a period of time and subsequently confirmed contracts worth a great deal of money. Even more importantly, the exercise resulted in a valuable database which could be refined before impending UK local government reorganisation – a situation where current intelligence was critical.

You, too, can achieve things at very little cost when you start out. Just look at your market, decide what you need to know, then find a way to get the information you require by simply *asking* for it.

ABOVE THE LINE PROMOTION

Above the line promotion means the kinds of promotion you buy in, for example to get a message across – for example advertising, PR and exhibitions. Let's consider them one by one.

Advertising
'Advertising' can have a very narrow, or very wide, meaning. It can easily mean expending an inordinate amount of money on exposure by sundry media activity: press, television, radio, hoardings and the like. For your first twelve months in business, you may well not need it. You will need to find some way of checking how much business (and profits) you actually achieve for each £100 of expenditure. If you don't budget sensibly, participation will cost you dearly and could bleed you dry.

Public or press relations

Nowadays to the cognoscenti this is often simply 'Relations'. Whatever, this is where you can really do yourself some good at next to no cost. Here's how:

- Identify the trade journals relevant to your enterprise and establish the editorial contacts for your area. Do the same with your local press media (including free sheets). The cost of a few telephone calls will elicit this information.

- Now make it your business to cultivate these new found contacts. Send a short press release to all of them about the launch of your enterprise and follow up this activity with personal introductions by telephone. Your strike rate first time around probably won't be very high but the important thing you will have achieved is contact.

- Keep up the good work with regular calls and releases on orders attained, new staff appointments and any other good news you can think of. These press contacts are going to be very useful to you for a long time to come.

The media are always on the lookout for news and if you continue to service them well, they'll eventually start coming to you as an authority for views on issues which relate specifically to your industry. All of this you can do for yourself without recourse to big ticket consultancies. It can also be a lot of fun.

Exhibitions

Depending on the nature of your business, public or trade exhibitions can be a great source of opportunity for the start-up. However, they can be quite costly and outside the range of most emergent concerns. If, on the other hand, you have a public sector marketing grant upon which to draw, and you know of a local exhibition which would help you, then do consider taking a small stand during your first year of trading. It can be a superb way of accelerating a company's database of prospective customers.

- Do you plan to advertise during the first year?
- Who will handle press and public relations for your business?
- Will you participate in local exhibitions?

CASE STUDIES

Tom and Paula plan their strategy

The initial marketing strategy for Tom and Paula's new enterprise is now well advanced. The entrepreneurial training programme has given both of them an insight into what marketing is really all about.

Conscious of his lack of experience in face-to-face selling, Tom has enrolled in a short government sponsored course on the science of selling. Meantime, Paula is devoting her energies to working out the overall marketing strategy, providing detailed guidelines on responsibilities for each of them.

Tom and Paula have decided that for the first year of operation their promotional activity will be restricted to producing a suitable brochure, and sharing a small stand at a local exhibition for the printing trade.

Paul and Hazel shop around

Hazel received a telephone call from The Junior Partnership requesting another meeting with both of them. The executive explained that she had been successful in obtaining a grant for them of £1,000 from a charitable trust who specialised in supporting innovative self-employment projects wholly devised and enacted by young unemployed persons. The remaining £500 would come to them by way of a soft loan from the Local Enterprise Trust.

When they got back home Paul secured a mobile van with a deposit and Hazel shopped around for a discount on a microwave oven.

Our young enterpreneurs were in business and it hadn't taken half as long as they had first thought.

'See, I told you we could do it.'

'Okay bighead. Sorry... Boss.'

Donation launches the business

With Mr Watling's generous donation to the 'Comely Coaches' venture, John and Colin were also in business. After another meeting with all the parties concerned, the contract with Social Services was signed. The community services project dreamed up on the bowling green was underway.

ACTION POINTS

1. Describe the essence of 'marketing'.

2. Show how you would set about developing a personal image for your enterprise.

3. List ways of acquiring cost-free publicity for your new business.

4. Draw up a Customer Charter for your enterprise, stating how you will greet them, how regularly you will call on them, how you will handle complaints, etc.

5. Draw up a similar charter for staff relations.

6. Jot down the most important things you don't yet know about your market. Devise a simple plan for essential marketing research. Then make a plan for your very first promotional campaign.

7

Cultivating the Selling Habit

You've produced a winning plan, you've got all your funding in position, your image is looking good, your brand new stationery still has the smell of printer's ink and perhaps you've moved into bright new premises already.

HOW TO BEGIN

- *You start from Day One developing the selling habit, and you keep on improving your sales sense until the day you retire or sell out.*

Even if you find it hard to acquire the selling habit to start with, after a while you'll discover that it is a very difficult habit to give up.

All you've been doing so far is setting up your stall and now you're about to embark on the biggest learning curve of your life. Even if you've been in sales for the whole of your career, you'll still be starting at square one because this time it's *all* down to you.

But what if your career path has been in a different direction altogether? What if you've never sold face-to-face before? How are you going to master the art in a short space of time?

The fact is that – whether you realise it or not – you've been selling face-to-face since the day you were born.

- Every time you negotiated for extra pocket money, you were selling.

- Every time you asked the boss for a salary increase, you were selling.

- Every time you talked your way out of trouble, you were selling.

LEARNING TO NEGOTIATE

- *What to remember when you're out there hustling is that you cannot actually SELL anything to anybody. They'll BUY from you, but only if they identify with* **you**.

That's precisely why getting *your* image right, right from the start, is the most crucial piece of marketing activity you'll ever undertake.

A formula to help you

But there must be some kind of formula for successfully developing the selling habit? There is. It's simplicity itself and it is adaptable to any situation. Let's examine this formula piece by piece, and then create a face-to-face scenario in the office of a potential customer whom you've never met before.

The selling formula

1. Prospect for your customers.

2. Make your appointments.

3. Clinch your deals face-to-face.

PROSPECTING FOR CUSTOMERS

As with all things in life, you must have a plan if you are to succeed. In this scenario, you want to provide yourself with a steady stream of prospects to buy advertising space in the range of local authority publications you will be handling. Here's your plan:

1. If the publication you have been assigned to is a 'repeat' (a second or third edition) then every advertiser in these editions is a prospect.

2. If it's a new publication, then any other recent handbook sponsored by the council will contain lots of prospects. It's a matter of simple common sense to determine those which are of particular relevance to your project – but consider them *all* as potential customers. Advertisers buy into these publications for all sorts of reasons which are not always obvious.

3. Look through the sponsored publications circulating in your catchment area. You'll see certain advertisers appearing again and again, even though there would seem to be no common link between the publications. These advertisers have multiple reasons for buying. Add them to your list.

4. Council supplier lists are an excellent source for prospects. Very

often you'll pick up sales from these suppliers for 'emotional' reasons, *ie* they are currently doing business with the council – or would like to.

5. Local newspapers, free sheets and *Yellow Pages* are also full of suitable prospects. Refer to them regularly.

6. If you are working out of a local authority office, cultivate your temporary colleagues. The book you are working on is very close to their hearts and they'll gladly help you in any way they can to provide you with potential customers.

7. Drive around the local trading estates and jot down the names of companies who fit the profile of your book. Add them to your list.

● *Apply yourself diligently to these seven steps each day and you'll rapidly build a database that will amaze you.*

MAKING YOUR APPOINTMENTS

A golden rule

You always use the telephone to 'sell the appointment' – not to make the sale! This is the cardinal error committed time and time again by the eager beavers going nowhere fast in the business of professional selling. Ours is a considered sale where the appointment is vital. We can then effectively demonstrate the product, sell the benefits, and clinch the sale.

Example

Hot prospects

From your accumulated prospects list, pick out enough 'hot ones' (say 30) to provide a pattern for your first week's appointments.

Territory management

Use the technique of 'territory management': arrange these in such a way that you could comfortably visit six per day (three morning, three afternoon) without risking a nervous breakdown.

Allocating times

Now make out lists for each day for these 'manageable' visits.

Against each prospect allocate an appointment time (9.30, 10.30, 11.30 *etc*).

You now have an ideal appointments pattern for the week ahead. 'But how I can possibly expect prospects to conveniently fit in with my schedule?' If you have such a plan prepared *before* you make your telephone calls, you'll be pleasantly surprised how many people do fit in. Sure, you'll have to make the odd adjustment now and again but nothing like as drastically as you would without a plan. Try it. It works.

Your calls record
Now take a sheet of plain A4 paper and rule it exactly as the specimen sheet on the opposite page. This is your 'Calls Record'. Don't be fooled into thinking that this is pedantic or unnecessary. It's not. You need to keep an accurate record of your calls to determine what your strike rate is in:

- getting through to prospects

- clinching appointments.

By filling in the 'Calls Record' as you telephone, you will find that your confidence grows and your strike rate gradually improves.

'D' = DIALS. You may have to dial several times before being connected. Log the dials.

'C' = CALLS. Your initial call may have only connected you to the switchboard. Your prospect may be out or at a meeting. Log the calls.

'CC' = CONFIRMED CALLS. You've made it through to the prospect. Log the confirmed calls.

Totting up these entries at the end of your call sessions gives you an assessment of your improving performance.

Now you're ready to make those calls
You've done your homework, you've got your 'Calls Record' in front of you and now you're ready to make those calls in a confident and relaxed frame of mind.

DATE	PROSPECT	D	C	CC	REMARKS
Mon 6 May	Fyfe Cement	1	2	1	* 10am Tues 7th
	MDC Windows	3	2	1	* 3pm Wed 8th
	Greyshom Dev.	1	1	1	Call back
	Campbell Const.	1	1	–	Closed for hols.
	Scotwest Plumbers	2	2	1	* 11am Wed 8th
	Midscot Training	1	1	1	Call back Thurs
	Shanks Printers	1	1	1	* 11am Thurs 9th
	Pioneer Builders	3	1	–	No response
	Tilcon Mortars	4	3	1	* 12.30 Fri first
	Loudon Plastics	4	2	–	Can't reach...
	Sullivan Signs	6	4	1	* 3pm Fri (will sign)
	Patterson Sols.	2	1	1	Not interested
	Thern Enterprise	2	1	1	* 2pm today (will sign)
	Tack Development	3	1	1	* 3pm today (will sign)
	Davidson Arch.	2	1	1	Call back Thurs.
	Dyke Workshops	4	1	1	Unavailable. Call back
	Bonnar & Co	3	2	1	Not interested
		43	27	14	* 8 appointments

CONVERSATION RATIOS FOR ONE DAY'S TELEPHONE ACTIVITY

CALLS	**63%**
CONFIRMED CALLS	**33%**
APPPOINTMENTS	**19%**

(i.e. 27 calls/43 dials x 100 = 63%)

Fig. 3. Example of 'calls records'.

All you need now is a draft script (**cue sheet**) to help you take charge of all your calls. You don't have to stick rigidly to it. In fact, it works better if you vary it according to how you instinctively relate to each individual prospect. Remember, no two people are alike, or react in the same way.

The cue sheet places you firmly in the driver's seat at the beginning of each conversation. Here's an example of the kind of cue sheet we use at Focus Publishing. It works well for us and you can easily adapt it to your own needs.

A scripted call
'Good morning, my name is Jim Green of Focus Publishing. We haven't met before but I was given your name as someone who might be interested in having their company included in the new edition of the Business Directory which Focus is currently compiling for X County Council. I'd like to make an appointment to come and see you. Would 10am tomorrow suit you? I promise not to take up much of your time – 15 minutes should do it.'

All this has taken no more than 30 seconds of relaxed delivery and already the prospect in question has been informed of:

- the caller's name

- the caller's company

- what the caller wants from the prospect (*ie* a brief appointment)

- when the caller *ideally* wants the appointment.

At this point any of the following can happen:

1. If the prospect's intrigued he'll agree to see the caller at the *caller's* appointed time.

2. If the date/time doesn't suit, he'll either suggest an alternative or ask the caller for one.

3. He may claim he's too busy to see the caller and ask for details by post or fax. The caller should desist from accepting this alternative, intimating that the proposition requires a brief personal meeting to do it justice.

4. The prospect may say 'get lost'. Depending upon his mettle, the caller can either accept that or try to convince the prospect that he's missing out on a good thing by refusing an appointment. (A good plan here is to hint that a competitor has already signed up.)

- Remember – what you're selling when you telephone is an appointment not the product or service. That comes later when you meet the prospect face-to-face.

CLINCHING A DEAL FACE-TO-FACE

Now you're here at the point of sale and there's no more exciting place to be for the committed professional. You've done your homework and secured an appointment. What's more, you've already gleaned some knowledge about your prospect's business, what it does and how it markets its product. Now you are going to impress the prospect with your knowledge.

In-and-out with a sale in 15 minutes
You're going to be in-and-out with an order in just 15 minutes and here's how you're going to do it:

1. Thank the prospect for agreeing to meet you and briefly (very briefly) introduce yourself and the company.

2. Describe the nature of your product or service and say how it will **benefit** the marketing of the prospect's enterprise.

3. Produce a sample of your product (or a fact sheet/brochure if it's a service). Explain in a little detail why it's so special, where it scores over the competition and how your prospect would benefit from doing business with you.

4. While you're doing this, handle your sample (or brochure) with tender care as if it were some precious stone. Then hand it to the prospect to touch, examine, browse through as the case may be. Watch out for **buying signals**.

5. Diplomatically answer any **objections** the prospect may raise.

6. ASK FOR THE SALE.

7. Complete the order, get it signed ... and leave.

Asking for the sale
Let's look again at 6 and 7 in more detail:

Ask for the sale
This is where
the eager beavers
invariably
fall down ...
It's simple.
Just **ask** for it
and if your presentation is good
you'll probably get it.
If not,
ask for it again.

This time
you'll get it.

Don't hang about
... and when you do
get your order ...
complete the details
swiftly but *accurately*,
thank your prospect for his business,
refuse a cup of coffee
and **leave**.

Hang about and you'll risk
talking yourself
out of the sale
in a fraction of the time
it took you
to make it.

Where the eager beavers fall down
The eager beavers ignore these five essential rules of negotiation:

- they're too keen (and it shows)

- they talk too much (unsettling the prospect)

- they ignore buying signals (they can't see them)

- they gloss over the benefits (going for an early kill)

- they make mistakes in their presentation (talking too much).

Don't be an eager beaver. Adopt the laid back, listening approach. Give the prospect a chance to talk, encourage him to talk. He'll tell you all about *his business*. He'll just love telling you about his business and then when you leave with your order, he'll tell everyone what a wonderful conversationalist you are. That's selling.

Avoid the rinky-dink sales approach
The rinky-dink is the 'no problem' merchant who causes no end of trouble for everyone else in the organisation. He will promise *anything* to land a sale and in the process lands himself in the drink. You can't afford to be like this. In the early days of your enterprise there will be no one else around to bail you out if you promise what you can't deliver.

Asking for 'yes' when they keep saying 'no'
You must always be prepared for a 'no'. Be philosophical about receiving 'no' for an answer and steely enough to go back again and again to convert a 'no' into a 'yes'. When you start out you'll have no track record, and will be looking for people to take you on trust. Don't let that put you off. 'No' doesn't necessarily mean 'no', as we'll discuss in Chapter 10.

Stripping away the mystique of sales
There's no mystique about selling. It's simply a matter of cultivating the science of negotiation, ensuring that every deal is done on the win-win basis: not just something for you, but something for the prospect as well.

THE TEN COMMANDMENTS OF SELLING

1. **Never fail to turn up for an appointment**
   If it's impossible to make it, telephone in advance advising the prospect why you can't be there on time.

2. **Never promise anything you can't deliver**
   If you do, you'll lose your integrity.

3. **Never knock the competition**
   Don't even mention them, let the prospect do that.

4. **Never argue with a prospect**
   You'll lose out if you do.

5. **Never leave a lost sale thinking it's lost forever**
   The deal may not have been right for him now but it may be later.

6. **Never turn up for an appointment reeking of alcohol**
   You're dead if you do.

7. **Never deviate from the purpose of the meeting**
   The prospect doesn't want to know what a wonderful person you are.

8. **Never take rejection to heart**
   You won't appreciate your wins until you've suffered the odd loss.

9. **Never be afraid to admit you blew it**
   You'll only be deceiving yourself if you do.

10. **Never fail to keep your sales records up to date**
    If you don't you won't get paid on time.

Successful people all love selling. It's the lifeblood of any enterprise. Get your act together, go out there are sell, sell, sell.

CASE STUDIES

Tom and Paula agree their sales policy

The marketing strategy has produced an agreed sales policy for the business and Tom and Paula have decided on the following:

1. The initial market will consist of Tom's previous contacts whom he has been calling on regularly and from several of whom he has

had requests for quotations.

2. The focus will be on pricing: not discounting but more of a value-for-money policy without impairing margins.

3. Paula will concentrate on new business development as an on-going project using telemarketing techniques from her home base.

Tom's course on the science of selling is already beginning to pay dividends. He feels much more confident in one-to-one situations.

Hazel's brainwave
'We'll have to think about some marketing, Paul. To get us up and running.'

'You what?'

'Marketing. Well, some leaflets then, I suppose. It's all we can afford.'

'Who are we going to hand them out to?'

'I've thought about that. School playgrounds for a start. Kids are always hungry. Remember how we used to be?'

'That chap at the "Junior Partnership". He said he could help us with leaflets.'

'Then let's call him, Paul.'

ACTION POINTS

1. Describe in detail how you will prepare for customer prospecting, making appointments and clinching the deals face-to-face.

2. Construct a script you'll feel personally comfortable with for face-to-face selling.

8

Developing the Right Qualities

Entrepreneurship calls for a strange, sometimes conflicting mixture of qualities but they are all essential in one way or another. The reason you must develop these qualities is so you can automatically shift up or down a gear as you face ever changing circumstances. This way you will always be in control.

SEVENTEEN ESSENTIAL QUALITIES

Place a tick beside those qualities you possess.

1. ambition   _____
2. persistence   _____
3. endurance   _____
4. obduracy   _____
5. understanding   _____
6. empathy   _____
7. articulation   _____
8. confidence   _____
9. decisiveness   _____
10. humour   _____
11. persuasion   _____
12. intuition   _____
13. temperance   _____
14. patience   _____
15. style   _____
16. service   _____
17. humility   _____

DISCOVERING AMBITION

Ambition

Unless you're chock full of this, you'll be sunk before you start. How high is your ambition? Do you want to be a millionaire in five years' time? Perhaps the accumulation of wealth is unimportant to you, and your ambition takes other forms – status, personal development, security, recognition by others.

The really important thing to establish before you set out on your journey is the extent of your ambition and in which direction it lies. Establish that early on and you can devote all your energies to achieving what you *really* want from your endeavours.

That's the critical mistake I made first time round. I didn't truly know where I wanted my ambition to lead me and as a result I paid a heavy penalty.

QUALITIES TO ADD STEELINESS

Persistence

Once you are clear where you want to get to, be prepared to persist until you achieve all of your goals. There is no point in putting so much work and effort into a plan if you fail to carry it out.

The real achievers in life are not necessarily captains of industry or high profile personalities; they are those ordinary people who go about their business quietly and persistently, ticking off each goal as it is achieved.

Your plans won't just fall into line, because things don't just 'happen'. You have to make them happen through persistent effort.

Endurance

Definition: n. 'power of enduring; bearing (hardship) patiently'. Notice the word in parenthesis. It's optional. Obstacles only become hardships when you allow them to. Much better to exercise your power and endure the obstacles you will encounter along the way until you find a way to turn them around into victories.

There's an old song which contains a famous line:

> There's no one with endurance like the man who sells insurance

... and there are many successful entrepreneurs in the insurance industry.

Obduracy

This is not a very desirable quality but you'll need a smidgeon of it in your make-up. There are times when you'll have to be really stubborn to get things done. Only be obdurate when you know for sure that what you believe is indeed the right thing.

You must also expect to be seen as hardhearted at times, as when you have to fire someone because they are fouling up the operation. People don't always see it your way.

RELATING WELL TO PEOPLE

Understanding

Expect to be asked for a great deal of understanding on your way to the top. People will expect it of you: understanding why the goods didn't arrive on schedule, understanding why customers can't pay you for another month, understanding why three members of the staff are all going on holiday at the same time – understanding all manner of things.

Whatever, don't lose your cool. The answer often lies in communication, or the lack of it. Listen carefully to what everyone has to say, then take your own counsel in resolving the situation. That doesn't mean steam-rolling. It means negotiating for a win-win result.

Showing empathy

Empathy goes a little deeper than simple understanding. It means developing the power to enter into and understand another's feelings without intrusion. True empathy takes a lot of patient practice but it will pay you handsomely if you perfect your technique. Never try it as a subterfuge, though; it will certainly backfire.

To exercise empathy you must be totally honest with yourself and the other person involved.

Being articulate

This does not mean talking like a BBC Radio 3 announcer with a plum in his mouth. It simply means expressing your thoughts very clearly in your own words, in your own accent, but in such a way that everyone can understand you. If you can do this efficiently all the time, you'll find it very helpful if called upon to engage in public speaking.

Displaying confidence

Confidence is a quality all entrepreneurs have or acquire, but not always in a way you'd notice. More often than not their confidence manifests itself as quiet self assurance which seems to inspire confidence in others.

Example
Take Richard Branson for example: nice young chap who apparently doesn't have a suit to his name yet controls multi-million pound empires casually (seemingly) with a unique laid-back approach to commerce. He's got all the confidence in the world and a genuine smile always at the ready to go with it.

Being enthusiastic

You'll have noticed that Richard Branson is also brimming with this quality, too. They go hand in hand: confidence and enthusiasm. You can't have one without the other. Even when your stomach is turning over and you feel the pits, you have to keep your enthusiasm boiling over. It's infectious, keeps others on their toes and will keep you at the top of the heap.

Being decisive

The entrepreneur never has a problem making a decision in any situation where a clear decision is called for. Because of his experience in looking problematic situations straight in the face, the entrepreneur can weigh up the pros and cons very rapidly and just as quickly come to a reasoned decision. The entrepreneur will stick by that decision when others around are expressing doubts.

Acting speedily

Akin to decisiveness is speed of action in every undertaking. You've heard the old adage, 'If you want something done in a hurry, ask a busy man.' This is not to imply that you should rush through your everyday tasks like there was no tomorrow. On the contrary, do all you have to do each day but do it in your own time on a wholly organised basis. This way you will prioritise your activities, perform them all efficiently, recognise instantly when something requires immediate attention and generally get yourself up to entrepreneurial speed calmly and effortlessly.

The need for humour

You'll need a pretty good sense of humour for the road ahead, which you will find is so often full of Dismal Johnnies. A well developed sense of humour will lift you well clear of so many emotional traps.

Persuasiveness
This is a very handy quality to have. You'll never (without employing undue pressure) get anyone to do anything they really don't want to do, but with gentle persuasion you can often get people to see things your way if they're hovering on the brink.

Example
Suppose you're selling cars. Tell the customer who wants the best part exchange terms that his car is exactly what you've been looking for, is in great nick for its year and is a credit to its owner. In short, make it clear that you're really pleased he came along. As a skilled business person you should have a bit of margin to play around with in the mark-up of the car you're trying to persuade him to buy.

Using your intuition
Intuition is a magnificent quality if you know how to use it properly. Call it what you will – intuition, creative thinking, inspiration, lateral thinking. You can't buy it, you can't rent it, but you can certainly develop it.

Good intuition is a matter of listening to and cultivating the inner voice. It's best accomplished when you're relaxing, your mind is unburdened and you have left the cares of the day behind. Try, it really works.

Remaining temperate
Keeping calm, and keeping a sense of proportion, are not always easy for those of us with a compulsive nature, but it's a quality it will pay you to develop in business. Being temperate means keeping moderation in all things, for example treating adversity with same equanimity as success.

Being patient
Whether you like it or not, you will need a great deal of patience if you are to be a successful entrepreneur – patience with your staff, patience with customers, patience with suppliers, patience as you wait for a result, patience in everything you undertake.

Developing your own style

You'll want bags of style as you promote your image as a budding entrepreneur. Develop style in how you dress, style in how you talk, style in how you walk and lots of style in handling sticky situations.

Learning to give good service

Of all the qualities listed in this chapter, giving good service to others is the catalyst which sparks off all the other qualities. All great men and women in history have exemplified the quality of service often without thought of reward. As someone in business, you are being *paid* to provide good service to others, so make sure you really do from day one.

Every day we all see endless examples of rotten service. Most of us simply put up with it because we think that's the way of the world. It's not. The business person who makes service to others a top priority will progress by leaps and bounds and leave the competition standing.

Example

The day before I completed this chapter I was having breakfast in a hotel in Worcester and had to ask three times before I got the pot of coffee I'd ordered some time earlier. The general level of service in that hotel wouldn't have passed muster in a shanty town in Nebraska let alone New York City. In the end, the patrons will simply spend their money elsewhere.

Humility

Do you think this is an unlikely quality for an entrepreneur? If so, perhaps you have yet to meet a real one. Humility is a word often misunderstood and misused. It has nothing to do with being walked all over; rather it means a genuine desire to be of service to others. It is the hallmark of the true entrepreneur.

SMOOTHING DOWN THE ROUGH EDGES

The foregoing represent the essential qualities of true entrepreneurship but there are others which you'll find expressed throughout the pages of this book.

Certain of these qualities you may already possess in abundance; others may seem alien to your nature. That's just a first impression and first impressions are not infallible.

For the next week or so concentrate on applying to your everyday dealings those qualities you feel easy with until their application becomes almost second nature. Then spend a full week working on each of the remainder. You won't find the work too difficult. This way you'll gradually smooth down any rough edges that might prevent you being successful in your journey of entrepreneurship.

CASE STUDIES

Tom and Paula progress their strategy
Let's have an update on how Tom and Paula are getting on:

The business plan is now complete and has been circulated to all potential funding sources.

They've had several more meetings with the public sector officials, and while it's slow going, they both feel sure that they're on the right track to securing funding assistance for the enterprise.

Tom's had a few more orders confirmed.

Paula has come to an arrangement with the Local Enterprise Trust whereby for a nominal fee (and without long-term commitment) they will rent accommodation facilities: occasional room hire, mail receipt and dispatch, message-taking, fax and secretarial services.

They have both been looking out for suitable permanent premises and have located some likely propositions.

All in all, they are reasonably satisfied with their efforts to date.

Hazel has the collywobbles
The night before the launch of their catering business brought on an unexpected attack of nerves in the normally unflappable Hazel. She was 'feeling the fear' for the first time and collywobbles were starting to get the better of her.

Paul came to the rescue with some words of soothing comfort.

'C'mon kid. This isn't like you, you've been a tower of strength for the past few weeks. We'd never have got this far without your staying power. It's going to be okay. You'll see.'

John and Colin learn not to assume
Day One of the 'Comely Coaches' venture proved eventful. John and Colin were only minutes into their first assignment when the fanbelt snapped. Fortunately, one of the senior citizens on board the coach was a retired mechanic and he volunteered to effect emergency repairs.

The management learned a timely lesson from the episode. As Colin put it, 'Never assume, always check. We'll have to pay more attention to preparation in future.'

ACTION POINTS

1. List the entire range of entrepreneurial qualities you will require to develop in order to be sure of success in your new venture.

2. Name the single greatest quality you can develop.

3. Now make out a list of your own personal qualities, then place them in the order of importance to you. Don't be coy about doing this. You've got good qualities in abundance but maybe you've never given yourself credit for them. Now compare your list with that of the entrepreneur, ticking off those that match. Look at what's left and then start working on them at your own pace.

9

Maintaining Progress

To ensure steady progress as you go about your business you must be confident in your ability to control the cash, to negotiate effectively with everyone you come in contact with, to devise strategies for success.

CONTROLLING THE CASH FLOW

Why cash is king

From the moment you start out on a business of your own you must develop the habit of controlling the cash; what you take in, what you pay out. It's called cash flow management.

Don't confuse cash flow with profit. Cash and profit are not the same. Profit includes a number of non-cash items such as depreciation and accruals (costs that you've included but not yet been invoiced for).

Cash flow on the other hand is a simpler concept. It's the balance between the cash you've received (from customers or other sources) less the cash you've paid out (to suppliers and employees). Businesses that go bust do so because they run out of cash, not because they are unprofitable. History records thousands of companies who made paper profits but went bust because they didn't control their cash.

Keeping a cash book

Unlike profit, you can calculate your cash flow at any point in time and do it very quickly. In fact, for the new business venture it is important that you know exactly every day how much cash your business has. This can easily be done by all non-accountants. You simply keep a **cash book** in which you religiously record each day the cash you have received (whether in cash and/or by cheque) and cash that you've paid out (whether in cash and/or by cheque).

There are a number of simple cash book formats available from stationery suppliers, most good high street bookstores and stationery retailers. Alternatively, your accountant will draw up a format that best suits your type of business.

Understanding your cash flow

To many people cash flow has to do with persuading a friendly bank manager to grant an overdraft facility which they've been conditioned to believe will rise and rise and that's the only way you stay in business. This is nonsense.

Getting the cash flow right from the start is critical and keeping it on the right track is even more crucial. But how can you do that if you're not yet self-financing? There is a way, a very sensible way.

● You must structure your business in such a way that the bulk of the cash comes in before you have to pay out. That way you'll be working on other people's money, interest free.

I've got such a business. For every project we undertake, we collect 70 per cent of the targeted revenue before we press the button to produce the product. There are many such businesses. Look around and you'll find one.

Keeping your books up to date

Ensuring that your books are always up to date should be a hands-on responsibility for either you or your partner, depending upon which of you possesses the required skills. You may well hire someone to physically 'write up' the books manually or electronically, but one of you should fully understand the process and be directing it. This way you'll always know how your cash flow is performing. Too many start-ups haven't a clue as to how they're doing and usually find out too late to remedy a bad cash flow trend. Don't let that happen to your enterprise.

The books you need

Once again the 'books' you require are simple. All businesses need a **cash book** and a **debtors ledger**. If you have a number of suppliers it's then important that you also record the relevant entries in a **purchase ledger** so that you can easily keep track of what you owe your supply sources and when payment is due. Depending on your type of business – *eg* manufacturing or contract work (plumber, electrician, builder *etc* – you may require a **job costing ledger**. The format and completion of this ledger is too involved to discuss here but do ensure that your accountant gives you a thorough briefing on the pros and cons of maintaining these essential records.

Remember, your books are your main source of information. They'll tell you

- how you are doing
- what cash you have
- what cash you need.

They are also required for inspection by a number of statutory agencies: namely the VAT man and the Inland Revenue, so always keep your books up to date. It's to your advantage in the long run.

Getting some ink on the books
Getting some ink on the books means getting some business in on a regular basis and the only way you'll achieve that is to be out looking every day. A neat set of accounting records may impress your auditor but it won't buy the groceries unless the books are covered in ink – black ink, recording sales transactions and money owed/received.

Hiring an accountant to audit your books
This must be one of your early assignments if you plan to trade as a limited company but look around carefully before deciding. I would recommend you stay away from the bigger practices and opt rather for someone who'll understand your teething problems. You need:

- Someone you can trust and get on well with.

- Someone who is established in your local area.

- Someone who is recommended to you by your bank manager, LEC, TEC or by a professional colleague.

- Someone who is adequately qualified to look after your interests.

Paying your way
By all means take credit (as much as suppliers will allow) but always pay your suppliers on the date you agreed between you at your first meeting. Do this and when the time comes when you need a little more time to pay, you're more likely to have your request granted. It's called trust.

Getting the cash in

I talked about this in some detail in an earlier chapter. If you've forgotten what I said, go back and read it again. Cash coming in less regularly than you're shelling it out spells trouble.

Don't help yourself to the till

In the early days of trading and especially if you are on a roll and the cash is flooding in, it can be very tempting to help yourself occasionally to the till. Avoid this at all costs. It's a mug's game and the only person you'll be robbing is yourself. Till dipping is the most dangerous habit the emerging entrepreneur can fall into because sooner or later you'll have to account for your light fingers and the people you'll have to account to are your creditors.

Trying to trade out of trouble

Trading out of trouble means taking on ever bigger amounts of new business in order to pay off old debts. This is a well-known road to ruin, because your total outstanding debts will simply get bigger and bigger. Avoid the temptation to 'trade your way out of trouble'. Concentrate instead on solving the underlying problems of the business.

NEGOTIATING SUCCESSFULLY

Every time you negotiate in your business dealings, try to focus on achieving a win-win result – every time. Win-win is good – good for everyone, particularly in a situation of negotiation for survival. Always leave the other person a door to walk in and out of – and some breathing space for yourself to reflect, gird your loins and get back into the action.

Too many business negotiations fall down because neither party is prepared to give way a little, usually from a sense of insecurity. Both sides are afraid of the outcome of giving away even as much as a penny. But what's there to be afraid of? There's always something you can give without suffering too much pain: even a gesture of showing willing or softening up your attitude can prove sufficient to resolve a dispute in a friendly way.

You'll have to develop this negotiating talent – not to be top of the heap but simply to survive in your chosen enterprise.

Negotiating to buy
When you're starting out it's no great problem negotiating the right terms for the furniture, computer equipment, pens, pencils, paper and so on that you're going to need to get you going. These suppliers are all engaged in highly competitive markets; they're just as hungry as you are even though they may have been operating successfully for many years.

However, no matter the nature of your particular venture, you'll need to find and then negotiate with regular suppliers who will be essential to the successful functioning of the business. It makes no difference whether you're manufacturing or supplying a service – locating and negotiating successfully with these essential supply sources is vital.

To begin with you'll have to depend heavily on your best asset, *ie* your integrity, coupled with a measure of personal charm. Even if you have a track record in your chosen trade or profession, you'll still have a job to convince regular suppliers that you're going to prove a good credit risk for future dealings.

Remember – particularly at the outset – that negotiation is a two way process. Give a little, take a little... and if you keep on doing that you'll be the one that gets more in every negotiation.

Negotiating to sell
We examined this concept earlier in Chapter 7. Before you read further, flick back for a quick recap on the basic ideas discussed here.

Making it happen
Many negotiations in the exhilarating arena of selling face-to-face falter because the person trying to clinch the sale fails to recognise that things don't just happen; you have to make them happen. Remember the essential work you have to do before you reach the face-to-face interview to get your order approved: researching, prospecting and appointment making. If you sit around too long waiting for inspiration, you'll find the main event slipping away from you to be quickly replaced by gloomy despair. Don't let this happen to you.

Example
This section of the book came together following a visit I made to the south east of England on the negotiation of future publishing contracts. I also managed the time to fit in several 'catch you up'

meetings with field sales personnel. One of these in particular inspired this section.

He'd been with the company for only a matter of weeks but his performance to date was quite outstanding. I told him so as soon as we met up but to my surprise he was full of moans and groans together with foreboding about the future. He'd had three good weeks beforehand but (even though it was only Wednesday) was now rapidly convincing himself that he was doomed to drawing a blank this week and worse still, that this was to be the pattern for all nine remaining weeks of the project he was currently working on.

My unhappy operative couldn't wait to let me know how bad things were: he had been assigned to a bad project; it didn't match the profile of the area; the area was much too vast for one man to get results; the results he'd obtained so far were all we could hope to achieve; achievement on the scale I was looking for was quite impossible; 'Impossible', his wife had told him the first day he started . . . and so on and so forth.

I listened to him whingeing for 15 minutes until I could stand it no more.

'So, what are you saying? You want out?'

'I didn't say that,' he replied. 'I'm not a quitter. I'll see the project through.'

'What's there to see through? You've convinced yourself that there's nothing left to go for.'

Claiming vehemently that he was not a quitter and wanted to be allowed to continue, he then proceeded to disprove *my* point about *his* assessment of the project, *ie* there would appear to be nothing left to go for (although he couldn't see for himself at the time that he'd actually done rather well and that there was still substantial room for manoeuvre). He'd certainly done his homework on *perceived* self destruction as he showed by producing reams of statistics in a further effort to convince me of the non-viability of what he was doing, culminating in a performance appraisal which looked like this:

Companies contacted to arrange an appointment....	172
'No's' by telephone	50
Outstanding call backs	36
Appointments booked	86 (176)
Appointments completed	73

Sales confirmed...	31
'No's' face-to-face or subsequently confirmed........	20
Still considering..	22 (73)

All in all his performance was acceptable measured against the benchmarks of this particular business. His problem was immediately apparent. 'No's' equalled failure and 'considering' represented future failure. He couldn't see the wood for the trees ahead and had decided that the end was nigh.

'You reckon that's it then, do you?', I said. 'Losers 7, winners 1. End of the game, take down the goal posts and go home.'

'No, no ... I was hoping that with your experience you'd find me a way back into the action.'

I looked at him in disbelief.

'Who do you take me for, son? Svengali, Houdini, one of those guys? You present me with what you regard as a scenario for disaster and you want me to show you the way out. How long have I got?...'

What we did then was to sit down and evaluate his moans and groans to establish which of them we could do something about and which weren't even worthy of discussion, ending up with an evaluation of his own performance appraisal.

What came out of the latter exercise was positive proof that he'd done rather well despite his misgivings and that there was plenty of room for improvement. The conversion factor of 42.47 per cent on confirmed sales to face-to-face appointments was excellent and I was able to persuade him that 'considering' didn't necessarily mean 'no' but rather perhaps 'maybe', 'not now', 'later'. We put this to the test that very afternoon. We called on six of these pending transactions and walked away with a further four sales to make his efforts for the week look more respectable.

'That was brilliant,' said my now re-invigorated operative as we left the last appointment. 'I wish I had your magic.'

'There is no magic. It's all down to application and negotiation. You'd have got those four sales by yourself if you'd been negotiating effectively.'

That's the truth of the matter as we found in the conversation that followed. After a few rebuffs earlier in the week he had fallen into the trap of convincing himself that 'no' and 'considering' equalled failure. He'd also lost sight of several options at his disposal for immediately turning round these initial reactions into confirmed sales: second advertisement colour thrown in free of charge, discounts and (but only as a last resort) deferred payment. The sales we obtained that afternoon were all clinched on painless negotiation: free second colour to seal an early deal.

Be prepared to negotiate every deal with the tools at your disposal when you are up against initial resistance.

Negotiating your selling policies

It's your privilege to create the policies that set your selling prices but always try to be flexible by negotiating with everyone connected with the process: with yourself on occasion. That's fine as long as the end result is the protection (or improvement) of your margins.

Marketing effectively through negotiation

When you've read this book in its entirety go back again and study Chapter 6, 'Marketing Your Enterprise'. Observe how the negotiation process runs through every strand of activity contained therein in the effective marketing of your business. No one expects you to be a marketing guru when you first start out but some wide boys you will meet along the way may try to take advantage of the learning curve you'll be on for some time.

Never take anything at face value. Always try to work out the true value of what's on offer through common sense and by consistently negotiating with admen, designers, printers and the like.

Negotiating with your bank manager

I recently attended a useful hour long seminar sponsored by the bank my company uses. It was aptly entitled 'How to Handle Your Bank Manager'. Basically it was all about effective negotiation *before* the problems arise. Negotiating with the bank manager *before* you need additional funding, *before* presenting downturned year-end accounts, *before* the need to extend the overdraft.

Negotiating for your cash flow

Always remember the absolute necessity of continuous negotiation with both your debtors and creditors in order to ensure a viable cash flow for your business. Unless you negotiate, your cash flow will always be at the mercy of both your customers and your suppliers. That sort of diminished control spells disaster in the long run (see page 100).

Negotiation through networking

Another useful way of extending your negotiation skills is through commercial networking; for example through:

- Rotary Clubs
- Chambers of Commerce
- Local Enterprise Business Clubs
- Trade Associations.

These entities are always on the lookout for additional recruits and if you are gregarious (and prepared to serve on committees) joining one that best suits your own field can yield dividends.

If you can get up on your feet and talk at a moment's notice on a variety of topics, you could also join the local speaker forum.

You could even write a book...

SUCCEEDING THROUGH STRATEGY

You'll not only ensure success for your new venture but you'll enjoy that success sooner than otherwise if you develop the practice of creating individual strategies for all your endeavours. Strategies for everything.

Making good use of your business plan

Your business plan is your very first attempt at strategic planning. It explains:

- what your idea is all about
- how it works in practice
- how you will set about raising the required funding
- what you'll do with the funding when you get it
- what profit levels you are aiming to achieve
- how you'll market your venture

and a whole manner of other essentials for successful trading.

Don't leave your business plan lying about gathering dust once you're up and running. Feed it into your word processor and discipline yourself to its regular updating. This plan is your core tool for strategic planning. Change and develop its contents in tandem with the progress of your enterprise. Don't leave it until the end of the year, or even quarterly. Update it at each month-end and if you can't find the time to do it yourself, delegate this vital task to your partner. It's no use popping in to ask the bank manager for additional funding three years hence with a three year old plan, even if you're doing exceptionally well. He'll just send you away until you get it up to speed.

Developing a strategy for everything

Over the years I've developed the habit of never undertaking *anything* in my personal or business life without first committing to paper a strategy for its successful conclusion. Properly constructed strategies are essential for efficiency: they establish what your purpose is in any undertaking, what you are planning to ultimately achieve and what you might be prepared to agree to in a tricky negotiation. Strategies also help you get there faster.

Strategies for everything? Surely that involves a great deal of time and effort? Not at all. Once you get the hang of it you can develop strategies on the back of an envelope, the blank space in the 'Stop Press' column of your evening newspaper or even (as I've done on many occasions) the reverse side of till receipts.

Strategies for tricky situations

When you're faced with a difficult piece of negotiation always turn up with your own carefully constructed strategy for resolving it effectively. You may think you've already got the answer in your head but if you fail to commit it to paper beforehand (just one A4 sheet will suffice) you may be in for a pasting. Chances are the other party has a written strategy secreted somewhere easily accessible in that bulging file.

What do you include in this single sheet of A4 to construct an effective strategy? – just the salient points will do. But set it out in such a way as to provide for easy reference, cross reference, balance and counterbalance as discussion ensues. You let your guard down every time you resort to raking through files to find a trump card.

Example
Let's take a hypothetical example and draw up a strategy to manage the situation:

You're about to place an order for £100,000 worth of essential equipment but you have an uneasy feeling about both the deal and the suppliers. You can't point to anything in particular as to why you should feel this way, but as you think about it there are one or two aspects that need clarification before you sign on the dotted line.

Here's what you do with your A4 sheet.

REDCAR ENGINEERING EQUIPMENT PURCHASE

Positive Factors

Negative Factors

1. Price seems fair (but could we negotiate for better terms or deferred payment?)

1. Service package too loosely defined. Needs clarification.

2. Sound company with 30 years' experience in the industry.

2. Don't feel comfortable with Production Director. Ask about his background. Find out how long he's been with the company.

3. Guaranteed delivery dates.

3. How strong is the guarantee? Ask for belt and braces security.

4. Only company around who can handle a job this big.

4. Is this *really* true?

Conclusion
1. We haven't done our homework thoroughly.
2. We had better get total clarification before proceeding.

Action
1. Hammer them for improved price and terms.
2. Don't commit until negative factors are eliminated.

Option
Leave the entire deal on ice for another month, while we source elsewhere.

Laying out the pluses and minuses in this fashion coupled with conclusions, potential action and options allows you to focus on the main menu while flicking back and forth for balance and counterbalance in your discussion.

Strategies for controlling meetings
Never ever engage in any meeting with anyone without first preparing a strategy for control. If you don't do this you are in

danger of being both rolled over and railroaded.

When anyone mentions the word 'meeting' to me I switch on automatically to a little list indelibly impressed on my conscious mind (although I do have a written version in my pocket in the event of a power failure). It goes like this:

- Who's calling this meeting?
- Why?
- What the *real* purpose behind it?
- What's on the agenda?
- Is there a hidden agenda I don't know about?
- What's in it for me?
- What's the best I could hope to achieve?
- What would I settle for?

Sounds suspicious? – but it pays to get as many facts together as you can before participating. This way you're more likely to be the one in control.

Strategies for success

Basically, every strategy you evolve as you go about your business affairs should be a strategy for success – otherwise there would be no point in bothering to produce them. In other words, your strategies must:

- be positive in their outlook
- examine problematic aspects objectively
- arrive at conclusions
- pose options
- suggest initial action.

If you keep at it, you'll soon find that strategy making comes naturally to you in your everyday dealings and that success comes sooner rather than later.

Strategies for survival

Even established concerns which have been successfully trading for many years can sometimes reach a stage when creating a strategy for survival suddenly becomes imperative. This can happen overnight for a variety of unforeseen circumstances: market evaporation, product obsolescence, price wars and the like.

This is unlikely to happen to you in the beginning but as you progress, always be prepared for the possibility.

You can develop strategies for any eventuality but here's one you might want to give consideration to if you haven't yet committed to starting out on your own. Maybe giving up your current career is a worry to you, maybe you just want to taste and see.

Strategies for piloting a new business

Constructing a strategy for launching a new business on a part-time pilot basis is something I wouldn't recommend lightly. However, since I recently completed that task for a friend, I will touch on it here. There is nothing wrong with piloting your venture in advance, as long as you treat the exercise as if it were to be your bread and butter without any jam on top.

Here are a few factors to bear in mind before committing yourself to a pilot operation:

- Refine your business plan accordingly.

- Don't allow for any external funding except perhaps from your bank manager who might be prepared to lend on a fully secured basis.

- Treat the following as if you were going full-time:
  - corporate image
  - market research
  - pricing policy
  - marketing programme
  - sales strategy.

- Consider carefully before opting to pilot from home on a part-time basis. The bank won't much like it and neither will your suppliers and customers. Your best route is to get a temporary base at a recognised business centre.

FEELING THE FEAR

As you walk the unfamiliar roads to starting an enterprise for the first time, it's only natural to feel the collywobbles taking hold now and again. But fear is only an emotion and if you understand and handle it correctly it can be useful to you.

That sinking feeling

You found your idea, you wrote a brilliant plan, your plan got you your funding, you launched your enterprise and here you are on your first day sitting at your brand new (secondhand) desk surveying your empire.

What are you feeling right now?

The chances are you'll have a sinking sensation in your gut and feel scared witless. Don't be alarmed. It's all part of the experience of entrepreneurship. The solution is to get off your desk, out of your office, meet lots of people and start selling. There is nothing like a few calls and a few early wins to settle you down. Leave as much paperwork as you can to your partner.

Every time you feel the collywobbles coming back, repeat the exercise.

The positive side of fear

Left to its own devices, even the slightest fear will very quickly turn into worry and worry eventually into panic. Identify your fears as they occur; look them straight in the eye and analyse them. They will relate to one of two things: things you can do something about, things you can do nothing about. Forget the latter and concentrate on that for which you can do something, *anything*, to put right.

This is the positive side of fear. Use it always and you'll have nothing to fear. At the height of the depression in the early 1930s President Roosevelt admonished the citizens of the United States with these words of wisdom, 'We have nothing to fear but fear itself.' He was right and went on to prove it, and gradually confidence returned.

Addressing problematic situations

Practise addressing problems as soon as fear arises, and very soon you'll find that you are not only addressing them confidently but solving them fearlessly and successfully.

Clearing the hurdles

There are truthfully very few hurdles you will meet in your journey of entrepreneurship that you cannot overcome somehow or other. In the beginning molehills can look like mountains. Just sit down, analyse the problem, discard the impossible and get on with that which can be done.

THE GOLDEN RULE OF PERSONAL INTEGRITY

Your personal integrity is, and will always remain, the *most vital* asset of the new enterprise you are planning to launch. This personal quality is more vital to you than all the funding you will raise, more vital than 100 confirmed orders to get you going.

Nurture and protect your integrity in all your dealings. What you say you will do, you must do – even if it costs you. If you make a mistake that produces a downside for someone else, put your hands up immediately and admit to it. Then do everything in your power to rectify matters.

Being honest with yourself

Above all, be honest with yourself. It's easy to convince yourself that things are okay when they're patently not. Address all of your problems as soon as they arise and deal with them with courage and integrity.

The secret of success in business is personal integrity. Everything else is down to application. Never forget that.

CASE STUDIES

Paula cautions Tom

Tom and Paula are on the home stretch now. The public sector funding is in position and they've even found a friendly banker who on the strength of their efforts to date is prepared to grant them an overdraft of £5,000 against an insurance policy on Tom's life.

The business has lift off, it's trading and the best is yet to come. Six weeks into the first phase of trading, Tom and Paula stepped back and reviewed their activities to date.

All in all, there was a lot to be pleased about: the order book was filling up, the first few completed projects had received critical acclaim from the clients and there had been no serious mechanical breakdowns.

However, Paula cautioned Tom that job costings would have to be looked at more carefully from now on as overall profitability was being impaired by some slack estimating.

Paul's wagon rolls

'All work and no play makes Paul a plonker. Let's take some time off, Hazel, and spend a few days away from the van. We can afford it now.'

And afford it they could as Hazel subsequently confirmed.

They talked to Hazel's dad that evening and he readily agreed to fill in for them while they were away.

The business had taken off, it was already into profit and the young entrepreneurs were learning that rest is as important as activity when you're running your own show.

Business booms for Colin and John

John and Colin had just left the offices of the Enterprise Trust following a review meeting on their progress. They were relaxing over a pint in the 'Feathers'.

'The business development people seem quite happy with the way things are panning out,' said Colin.

'Yes,' replied John. 'Else they wouldn't be talking about introducing us to some possible new contracts. If we carry on at this rate we'll both be back on PAYE before too long...'

ACTION POINTS

1. Pinpoint exactly when the collywobbles are first likely to strike you in your enterprise.

2. Highlight the positive use you can make of feelings of fear.

3. Describe how you will tackle problematic situations.

4. Place a value on your personal integrity in business.

5. Write down all the things you reckon might cause you most anxiety about setting up in business for yourself. Carefully examine each of them in detail. If you spend some time on this exercise, and do it calmly, you will find yourself providing most of the answers before discussing the matter with anyone else. Those that defy an acceptable solution, leave aside for a while, then try another way around or ask a fellow professional for advice.

10

Powering Your Way to Success

There are several things you can do to accelerate your progress and power your way to success. The tools you will need won't cost a penny: you already possess them. They are all within you and just waiting to be asked. These tools are priceless and they are yours to use whenever you please. Access is easy because they are all in your mind.

YOUR SECRET POWERS

Maximising your mindpower

Human mindpower is awesome. We all live in a mind world; how each of us sees in our mind's eye just what's happening out there in the real world actually makes it how it is. We look at the world through our eyes and immediately make judgements solely on the evidence of our eyes. In other words we start interpreting situations as soon as they occur in our lives. If we're not careful, mindpower can work against us if we fall into the bad habit of always looking for negative aspects in our daily experiences.

Try always to use mindpower effectively by the continuous application of positive thought and action. Events rarely 'are' as they seem, so wouldn't it pay you to look for the good in every situation?

Napoleon Hill, the American entrepreneur and author, is credited with the famous saying, 'What the mind can conceive and believe, the mind can achieve.'

Maximising your brain power

Your brain is equally awesome, more awesome than the most powerful computer ever invented or still to be conceived. It can translate into action all your ideas, and achieve your every scenario, ambition, and daydream.

Those who know about such things reckon that on average we use only one tenth of this power in finding our way around life. How much more efficient we would all become by increasing this percentage by just another five points.

Try maximising on your brainpower in every aspect of your new venture.

Drawing on the power within
Your mind operates on three distinct levels:

- conscious
- subconscious
- superconscious (or supraconscious).

We all know about the first two but what do we know about the third level? Very little by all accounts. What is known, though, is that those who develop the power of drawing occasionally on this level of consciousness open the floodgates to inspiration and prosperity.

Many people can testify to having occasionally touched upon the wisdom of the superconscious and so brought a little magic into their lives.

There are some excellent books available on the subject of mind power. Investigate for yourself, and start drawing on this power within yourself.

Drawing on spiritual energy
Call it what you will but there is an energy available to you, an energy generating through God, the Universal Force, the Power or whatever else you might wish to call it. Drawing upon this spiritual energy is easy although it does require continuous application on your part.

You owe it to yourself and to those around you to make the best of yourself, your mind and your brain. Life has a wonderful way of rewarding those who use their best endeavours in all they undertake.

Using your mindpower to overcome
No matter what your age or personal circumstances you can effectively use the magic of mindpower to achieve whatever targets you set yourself.

I had to rely almost entirely on mindpower when planning the launch of my company. I had no money, no resources, no income; and it looked as if my future was already behind me. I would have been sunk, unless I had developed a mind-set fixed firmly to achieving the targets I'd set myself.

Is age the problem?
Far too many people get hung up on the vexing question of age. How old (or how young) do you feel? That's how old or young you are, no more, no less. Of course you will meet prejudices along the way but what of it? Your age in numerical terms (and that's really all people are bothered about) is nobody's business but yours. Saw a few years off, if that makes you feel more relaxed, but never ever add any on, even if you think you're too young. Confusing, isn't it?

Use mindpower to set your *real* age in terms of maturity and then get cracking by using mindpower and precious time in tandem to achieve your dreams.

Is money the problem?
'Well, of course it is!' I can hear you saying. Isn't it always? But remember, your mind can work miracles. So, if shortage of cash to get you going is the problem, put your mind to work on finding a solution. There's no shortage of money in this world, just a void of information on locating it when you really need it. Let go, and let your mind lead you to it.

Is rejection the problem?
Don't allow constant rejection to get you down. It's a waste of time and energy. Fix your mind on what *you* want, and not on what *they* won't allow you to have. Remember, we live in a mind world. Make sure the environment in your mind is healthily compatible with your ambition and desires.

Is redundancy the problem?
If redundancy is the problem, then do as Tom did. Do something about it. Use mindpower to get you where you want to be. If no one else has the foresight to hire you, put your skills and that great mind to work to set yourself up in a profitable business of your own.

Is frustration the problem?
Did you retire too early? Are you in a secure salaried position but bursting to get out on your own? Frustration can eat away at you like a cancer. Don't allow it to happen to you. Get your mind on the case.

MOVING MOUNTAINS

As you are going through the initial machinations of convincing people about your business plan, attracting the interest of public sector funding sources and the banks, finding a suitable partner and locating premises, you may have to nudge the occasional molehill to get what you want.

When you are up and running and have been trading successfully for some time you will sometimes find yourself facing several mountains that require moving at once, or several doors to push open.

The three sisters of success

The tools you will need for these monumental tasks are the three 'Sisters of Success': faith, hope and love.

By faith, I mean boundless belief in human potential – not only your own potential but that of all the people you will meet and deal with in your business life.

Whatever else you may risk losing on your journey of entrepreneurship, you must never lose hope. Hope will see you through all the toughest and worse situations. Some of the most powerful stories in human life concern the triumph of hope over adversity.

And love? – what has 'love' to do with business? Love means placing the highest value on everything and everyone. You'll need lots of this if you're going to build a business that you and everyone around you will be proud of: love of hard work, love for your employees, love for your customers, love for your suppliers, even love for your competitors, and a love of the person you wish to become.

ARE YOU READY?

We are approaching the end of this short book which I hope has provided an insight into what it takes to start your own enterprise, regardless of age, circumstances, money, retirement, rejection or any other obstacle. Here now is a candid quiz to help you discover whether you've got what it really takes.

A self-assessment questionnaire

1. Does the sun only shine for you when things are going well? ☐

2. Can you handle adversity as well as success? ☐

3. Will borrowing to invest in yourself put you off your sleep at night? ☐

4. When people say 'no' can you go back again and ask for a 'yes'? ☐

5. Would you sacrifice your social activities in the quest for excellence? ☐

6. Do you find something (anything) good in everyone you meet? ☐

7. Are you easily offended? ☐

8. Will you freely share your expertise with those you employ? ☐

9. Do you always admit to your mistakes? ☐

10. Could you start again if it all went down the pan? ☐

To score
Score 0 if you answered 'yes' to questions 1, 3 and 7, and 3 points each time you said 'yes' to all the others.

Assessment
0 – 24: You are not really ready for the challenge.

24 – 27: Work on yourself – you can make it.

30: You can and will make it.

Total mastery of the ten elements that comprise the questionnaire is vital to:

- launching a successful enterprise
- developing it from strength to strength
- getting rich
- getting lots of fun out of it in the process.

Analysing your score

Does the sun only shine for you when things are going well?
If so, then in the words of a very old song, you've got to develop the habit of looking for the silver lining in every cloud. Things are rarely as bad as they seem. It's a case of (in the words of another old song) accentuating the positive and eliminating the negative. Positive thinkers are winners. Negative thinkers are losers.

Can you handle adversity as well as success?
Being in business for yourself is a whole way of life. It is full of peaks and troughs, successes and failures. The winners handle every outcome, good or bad, with the same equanimity. Winning is great, losing is awful, but neither experience is the final word. When you fail to make a sale or tie up a contract, ask yourself why. You'll learn something to your advantage which will make you much better able to succeed next time.

Will borrowing to invest in yourself put you off your sleep at night?
You may be lucky enough not to have to borrow to start off, but somewhere along the way you may have to borrow in order to expand. Does the prospect of that worry you? Think hard about it before you take the plunge.

When people say 'no' can you go back again and ask for a 'yes'?
When people say 'no', they very often mean 'not now' or 'later maybe'. In other words, they weren't ready for whatever reason when you asked them. Always be prepared to go back and ask again for a 'yes'. The worst than can happen is you get another 'no'. Then go back yet again and ask for a 'yes'.

How far would you sacrifice your social activities in the quest for excellence?
You might be surprised how many people wouldn't sacrifice any. If you go about things the right way you'll have so much fun doing business with people that you won't have a lot of time left for pure 'socialising'.

Do you find something good in everyone you meet?
Even the worst of us have merits in our make-up. Practise finding something of value in everyone you meet. It has much to do with the ability to communicate with people at every level. If you do not feel

very good at this, work on it. You will need this ability to succeed.

Are you easily offended?
There is nothing intrinsically wrong if you are, but you're going to meet one or two nasties along the way and you've got to learn how to deal with them. Look for the 'good', and if that doesn't work, rise above events. Whatever, never lose your cool.

Will you freely share your expertise with those you employ?
Lots of employers won't, as a matter of misguided principle. But if you're going to develop fully, you're going to have to share your expertise. You'll run the risk of having someone trying to steal your intellectual property (it rarely comes to anything) but it's a risk well worth taking.

Do you always admit to your mistakes?
You'll be found out pretty quickly if you don't. Be really honest and open in all your dealings with customers, staff and suppliers alike. Personal integrity is your prime asset. You must always protect it.

Could you start all over again if it all went down the pan?
I did, and I can tell you this; I came out of it a stronger and better person. If (God forbid) it happened again, I would certainly make another comeback. Could you?

Success, after all, is only failure turned inside out. Good luck!

ACTUAL CASE STUDY

Here now is an *actual* case study to help you assess for yourself how all the pieces discussed in the previous chapters actually fit together in a real start-up scenario. The only such case study I'm familiar with is my own, so let's have a look at what occurred in my situation over a 13 month period in the build-up to the business taking off.

Month 1: at the starting point
- plan of action determined on the day of redundancy
- visits to Natwest and Barclays to obtain their Start-Up Packs
- the first strands of the business plan begin to take shape
- work begins on company aims, name and logo.

This was a very difficult time for me: personal tragedy coupled with a severe lack of basic funding didn't make for an ideal start to my adventure. However, the steely qualities in Chapter 8 (in particular persistence and obduracy) saw me safely through the starting gate.

Month 2: progressing the plan

- progression of business plan
- initial outlines for profit & loss and cashflow
- search begins for information technology tuition
- start sourcing refresher course on entrepreneurship.

Applying myself to the development of the business plan was both therapeutic and a labour of love but I struggled over the financial projections and had to resort to some wild blue yondering. Sourcing the tuition I badly needed was a bind at the time but persuasion paid off in the end. Other essential qualities employed: ambition and endurance.

Month 3: putting the wheels in motion

- find, enrol on and start 13 week information technology course
- accepted for entrepreneurship programme
- initial appointments with small business advisers (Natwest/ Barclays)
- initial contact with public sector funding sources
- first draft of business plan completed.

The activities listed above were enacted with speed of application and successfully accomplished with the help of several other essential qualities: persistence, persuasion and decisiveness.

Month 4: tapping on the doors of the funders

- approaches to more banks for commercial funding
- technology training, all day Monday to Friday
- entrepreneurship programme, two evenings weekly
- second draft of business plan completed.

Month 4 was a period of hard slog when I knew for sure that nothing tangible was about to happen for quite some time. The keynote quality required was patience.

Month 5: identifying an equity partner

- identify future equity partner
- revamp elements of business plan

- partner produces realistic financial projections
- identify essential suppliers
- first major public sector funding meeting
- search begins for premises.

The hard slog continued but I could see several pieces of the jig-saw beginning to shape up which enabled me to move up a gear, emboldened me to progress the masterplan more quickly than I had imagined some months before. Qualities that helped: persistence, decisiveness and confidence.

Month 6: looking for premises
- complete the technology course
- premises search continues
- second public sector funding meeting
- ·start calling on potential customer base
- company incorporated.

No gargantuan strides forward quite yet but enthusiasm for the project was beginning to take over and the brick walls ahead didn't look too tough because the adrenaline was starting to flow.

Month 7: seed capital
- £10,000 seed capital secured (loans against insurance policies)
- minor breakthrough on funding. £3,000 DTI grant approved
- final version of business plan completed
- public sector funding meetings intensify
- presentation to LEC (Local Enterprise Council)
- entrepreneurship programme ends.

Still a long way to go but I felt I'd grasped the nettle and it wasn't stinging too badly. My confidence was growing daily and I was becoming more and more articulate in presenting the case for my project.

Month 8: knockback from the banks
- temporary accommodation arranged with government agency
- knockbacks from all banks approached
- intensify customer calls activity.

Locating an accommodation facility was a bonus and the initial thumbs down from the banks neither came as a surprise nor worried me. I was beginning to enjoy being back out there in the field again sowing the seeds for future action with my old customers. Playing its part during month 8 was persuasion coloured with a touch of style.

Month 9: first piece of business
- start trading
- invitations to tender on several projects
- first contract won
- further meetings with public sector funders.

Things were looking good now: up and running, tangible interest from the prospective clientele, a definite order and some sniffing around on the funding front. My confidence was starting to soar.

Month 10: swings and roundabouts
- invitations to tender on two major assignments
- customer calls intensify
- more public sector meetings (seem to be going backwards)
- knockbacks from all Month 9 tenders
- start discussions on strategic alliance with print house in the event of failure to attract sufficient funding.

Month 10 began brilliantly... and then wouldn't you just know... There was a major project ready to start immediately but where was the funding to see it through to fruition? A little panic set in causing a decision to instigate preliminary discussions on a strategic alliance with an established print house. Thankfully nothing came of this. The quality that saw us through: obduracy.

Month 11: time to worry
- ominous silence from all funding sources
- reject offer on strategic alliance
- extend catchment area on customer calls.

Time to worry indeed. We'd done everything right, we had an order of sufficient worth to prove our initial viability but still we couldn't get the funders to move. Patience, persistence and endurance were called for.

Month 12: major contracts confirmed
- first major contract confirmed
- second major contract confirmed
- start pressurising funders for decisions

- zero in on smallest of funding sources
- £5,000 'booster' loan approved.

Continued prospecting, appointment making and face-to-face selling resulted in pulling off another two big deals in the early part of Month 12 which motivated my partner and me to lean heavily on the funding sources. The first breakthrough here was due entirely to persistence.

Month 13: lift off...
- third major contract confirmed
- £20,000 of 'soft' loans approved
- £18,000 of grants approved
- overdraft facility confirmed
- move into new premises
- increase staffing
- business lifts off...

And so it came to pass... but without consistent use of the essential qualities discussed in Chapter 8, I don't think we'd have made it. Heavy stuff, but we got there in the end. If you believe you can do it, you will. It's all down to dogged persistence.

LOOKING TO YOUR FUTURE

Even as you're planning for the initial launch you should still be giving some thought to the future of your enterprise. It's never too early to start.

Profitable day-dreaming
A little creative day-dreaming can yield a rich harvest if you practise it on a regular basis.

An interviewer once asked the jazz musician Duke Ellington to explain the secret behind his prolific songwriting output over 60 years. Duke replied, 'Oh, I dream a lot. I got a million dreams. I've been day-dreaming since the day I was born.' Day-dreaming sharpens our focus on creativity and often accelerates the process to actuality.

Duke Ellington composed his famous *Mood Indigo* in just 15 minutes while his mother was cooking dinner. That was in 1931. *Mood Indigo* is still being played today, recorded and sold in big numbers as cassettes and CDs – not a bad result for a day-dream of over 60 years ago.

Scenario-planning

Few of us will ever be able to use Duke Ellington's facility for turning dreams into reality to such great effect but what we can do is to take our day-dreams and use them for a little scenario-planning.

What is scenario planning? We all do it all the time. It's also called the 'What If' game. What if I did this or that? What if I made a radical change to my pricing policy? What if I offered added value to the service I'm providing? What if I revolutionised my marketing programme? What if I decided suddenly to retire and lie in the sun? What if...

Scenario-planning means making a conscious assessment of how your day-dreams could work out in reality. Try it, it's fun.

Expanding your enterprise

There will come a time not too far away when you will start thinking about expansion. It may be expansion on a small scale, or on a grand scale. Whatever, you'll find scenario planning very helpful in determining which way you want to go and when.

Expanding through franchising

Many new business ideas which have traded successfully have eventually expanded dramatically through franchising. Franchising has played a big part in the development of such names as Coca Cola, Hilton Hotels and a host of well known firms in everything from fast food outlets to vehicle service centres. If your idea is simple to operate and could be replicated by suitably trained others throughout the country, you ought to examine the possibility of franchising as the means to future growth. Typically the franchisor develops a brand name backed by national advertising, and sells licences to independent franchisees to offer the service locally. The franchisor gets his profit from a mixture of lump sum payments and royalties or commissions on sales.

Expanding by trading in Europe

If your expansion plans are on a grander scale, find out as much as you can about what it takes to trade successfully in Europe. There couldn't be a better time to investigate than right now.

Right now there is a lot of money available from the European Union to help you get a business footing in the region. It comes in shape of grants and loans for expenditure on matters such as trade visits, research and product development. Investigate now.

Expanding internationally

How far you can travel in expanding your markets is only restricted by how far your ambition can travel. Look into the future now – how far do you think it would lead you, if everything went tremendously well?

ACTION POINTS

1. Find out what help is available for breaking into Europe.

2. Take a sheet of paper and jot down how you envisage your venture will have progressed in (a) five years' time, (b) ten years' time. Examine all the positive possibilities: expansion, franchising, overseas trading, selling out or hanging on in. Have some fun with this exercise without letting your imagination run riot. Mix practicality with a touch of wild blue yondering. Put your lists aside for a month or so, allowing osmosis and catharsis to take over. Now look at them again and you'll find yourself improving on your original outlines. Try it, it works.

11

Launching a Home-Based Internet Business

The growth of the worldwide Internet is phenomenal and its propensity to create money-making home-based business operations is equally staggering.

In the United States of America there are now over two million such operations. A few of these are generating millions of dollars in revenue, many have a turnover in the hundreds of thousands, and the bulk of the remainder produce sufficient sales to cover expenses and return a tidy but acceptable level of profit.

- How does one go about launching a home-based Internet business?

- Where do you start?

- How do you research the market?

- Where do you find the opportunities?

- What about start-up costs?

- Is it better to stick with one opportunity or hedge your bets with several?

- What are the available options for promotion?

- Do you need to be an experienced webmaster to succeed?

- Which levels of Internet expertise are essential?

We'll look at some answers to most of these questions in this brief chapter.

ENTERING THE FASTEST GROWING INDUSTRY IN THE WORLD

The Internet is the fastest growing industry in the history of the world and yet it is still in its infancy, offering even the novice an opportunity to build a home-based business, and compete with major corporations around the globe.

When you portray a professional image as a networker on the world wide web, no one need ever know whether you're operating from a skyscraper or doing your thing at a rickety desk at a window overlooking the village green.

Anyone with a suitable computer can be successful on the Internet with the proper training. All it takes is a willingness to learn and a desire to succeed. With these elements in position, you can begin to build a business for yourself that will help you to achieve your financial goals and independence.

- If you are new to the Internet and business on the Internet, this chapter should help you decide whether Internet marketing is for you.

- If you are already in business, read on and hopefully you will improve your skills *and* increase your income.

Good fortune awaits you on the Internet

There are riches available on the Internet but the reality is that it takes time and effort to build a business. You should start thinking in terms of what £50, £100, or £200 extra a month in your pocket could do for you. For most people, these amounts can mean taking an overdue vacation, or the extra cash needed to meet the monthly mortgage repayments without anxiety, or the money needed for repairs to the family car.

An extra £50–£200 a month is not only possible but also probable in a short period of time if you are willing to learn. It won't happen overnight, but six figure incomes are possible if you are willing to apply yourself for 3–5 years. You either have already seen or will see numerous advertisements on the Internet saying things like, 'Make £5,000 a week doing virtually nothing,' but this statement is unlikely to be true. As with any type of business, success takes time and effort.

WHICH TYPE OF INTERNET BUSINESS WILL YOU OPERATE?

Working from home, there are basically only two options at your disposal.

1. Selling your services as an expert or consultant in a designated field of commercial activity.

2. Representing a global concern as an affiliate reseller of their produce.

Let's focus on the latter option because this is the area where most worldwide home-based networkers operate and where the opportunities would appear to lie for making the most money.

WHAT EXACTLY IS AN AFFILIATE RESELLER PROGRAMME?

Simply this: many companies and webmasters will provide you (usually free of charge) with a personalised web site to sell their goods and services. Every time someone visits your site and makes a purchase, you are paid a commission. You can earn even more by actively recruiting other affiliates under you, receive additional commission for this, and enjoy *incremental* income from their efforts.

YOU'RE IN GOOD COMPANY WHEN YOU GO IT ALONE ON THE WEB

Operating as a home-based Netpreneur is a solitary occupation but you will be in good company because there are millions like you out there in cyberspace. Very soon it won't seem so lonely. You'll strike up friendships with all sorts of people you are unlikely ever to meet in person and you will experience generosity on an unbounded scale. You will be the receiver of freely given advice and practical assistance by way of affiliate programmes, web sites, virtual office suites, bulk mailers, domain name services, ezines, mailing lists, email facilities, autoresponders, ad submission tools, etc. – for which you will not be asked to pay.

This is the wonder of operating as an international networker.

Show willing, and you'll get lots of help and encouragement in your quest for success.

Can you think of any other business where you'd get all these just for the asking?

- **Free affiliate programmes** (to resell top-of-the-range produce globally).

- **Free electronic secure ordering systems** (to save you qualifying for merchant status).

- **Free web sites** (to help you build and promote your business).

- **Free virtual office suites** (to set you up as a cyberspace specialist).

- **Free bulk mailers** (to post your promotional emails to prospects).

- **Free domain names** (to personalise your email addresses).

- **Free ezines** (to enhance your knowledge through electronic training magazines).

- **Free mailing lists** (to send announcements to targeted groups).

- **Free email facilities** (to cascade your marketing activities).

- **Free autoresponders** (to reply instantly and automatically to worldwide enquiries).

- **Free ad submission tools** (to blast out your ads to millions at one click).

Which are the popular areas of opportunity?

Here, in an approximation of popularity, are the top dozen affiliate reseller opportunity categories on the Internet:

1. Wealth creation.
2. Communications.
3. Internet training.
4. Electronic publishing.
5. Software programmes.

6. Educational programmes.
7. Online shopping malls.
8. Personals/dating services.
9. Credit card facilities.
10. Banking.
11. Gaming.
12. Books (in hard copy format).

EVALUATING THE BASIC SKILLS YOU WILL REQUIRE

You do not need to be an experienced webmaster to be successful in your home-based Internet operation – quite the opposite in fact. Too much knowledge might only serve to get in the way of free-flowing creative expression.

However, there are several basic skills you will need to master. Hopefully though, it is safe to assume that you already possess sufficient expertise in most of them, the others you can pick up as you go along.

What are these basic skills?
- Acceptable levels of literacy, numeracy and articulation.
- Computer literacy.
- Rudimentary understanding of what the Internet is all about.
- Basic typing skills.
- Proficiency in receiving and sending emails.
- Ability to compose compelling sales copy.
- Working knowledge of the autoresponder facility.
- Competence in using electronic advertisement tools.

WHAT ABOUT START-UP COSTS?

The good news is that they should amount to very little. This is because of all the freebies you can locate on the Internet: free affiliate programmes, free web sites, free electronic tools for your promotional activities.

See Appendix 2 for details of where you can find these examples:

- 30 free-to-join affiliate reseller programmes
- 20 free email facilities.

The really good news is that they will almost all come to you completely free of charge if you access the URLs provided.

WHY MLM ISN'T A DIRTY WORD ON THE INTERNET

In conventional networking the term MLM (multi level marketing) has certain unfortunate connotations attached to it. Not so on the Internet. In fact MLM forms the backbone of all the affiliate reseller programmes you will encounter in searching for opportunities. If you decide not to participate in multi level marketing in your home-based Internet operation, you won't make very much money.

In cyberspace e-commerce, one sale leads to another because what you will be doing in effect is replicating your own efforts many times over (through others) as you go about building your downlines. That's the way it works on the Internet and that's why all of the major programmes encourage and foster MLM among their affiliate members.

The benefits are threefold:

1. You build your downlines without ever having to interface with the participants.

2. You are credited with a percentage of their earnings on levels scaling from 1–10 according to the nature of individual propositions.

3. You are relieved of the responsibility of collecting monies personally because the programme contractors handle that onerous task and remunerate you monthly by cheque or direct debit.

All the time you are also earning in your own right through your own personal promotional efforts.

- MLM is good for your Internet business.
- Make money from your own promotional activities.
- Build your downlines effortlessly.
- Earn additional income on a range of affiliate levels.

DOING DESK RESEARCH BEFORE YOU SOURCE IN CYBERSPACE

It will pay you to undertake some minimal desk research before you embark upon cyberspace sourcing. Not to find the bizops, but to enhance your appreciation of the sheer scale of the facilities available to you on the Internet. You can best achieve this by referring to the publications listed in More Business Books to Help You (page 189), most of which you ought to be able to borrow from the Internet section of any main or central public lending library. Use their photocopying services while you're there to copy any material of particular relevance.

When you are ready to start searching in earnest for opportunities, the Internet itself is the place to go first. Another excellent source is to be found in the content of your incoming emails (which will increase in number as you progress) and especially those from other networkers trying to interest you in their own propositions. Do not discard any of these until you have read them, many will contain gems of opportunity you might otherwise miss.

ACTION POINTS

1. Describe the desk research you would undertake before contemplating entry into a home-based networking operation.

2. Explain what you understand by the term 'affiliate reseller programme'.

3. Determine why funding is not a major issue when setting out to launch a modest Internet business which is to operate domestically.

4. List the entire range of electronic tools you would require.

5. Establish right now whether you would be suited to this type of business by going to the Appendix and investigating the various affiliate reseller programmes available on free offer.

AFFILIATE
NETWORK

If you have a web site, you can begin selling books, magazines, software, and other barnesandnoble.com products today! Reach the millions of people who are already buying products online. Here are just a few of the reasons to join the barnesandnoble.com Affiliate Network:

Build a Better Site

Suggesting products and promoting them on your site makes your site richer and keeps visitors coming back! We give you the easiest and most powerful tools in online commerce for use on your site. Link to millions of book, magazine, or software titles; link to our bargain and out-of-print stores as well as to our bestseller lists and promotions. You can even add our search box right on your site. There's no easier way to add e-commerce to your web site.

It's Easy and It's Free

There's no charge to participate. In fact, we pay you! Every time a customer you refer buys from our site, you earn a percentage of the sale. The tools we provide on affiliate.net make it easy to add commerce to your site, and our online reports let you track every sale, every day. When your visitors follow those links and buy from us, we'll pay you a percentage of the sale. We process the order, ship the products, and handle billing and customer service. It's that easy.

Make Money

Earn up to 7% on books, out-of-print books, magazines, music, and 5% on software, videos, and gift certificates. There's no limit to how much you can earn, and every single product we sell qualifies for commissions -- no exceptions! The more you sell, the more you earn.

Sell Books, Software, and Magazines

You earn a commission on every product we sell! And by linking to an online store with more products, you give your visitors more to choose from and get more opportunities to earn commissions for your site. Even if you link to books and a user buys magazines, you'll get a commission on everything they buy.

The Name More People Know and Trust

Customers want to buy from a name they trust. When you link to barnesandnoble.com, you send your customers to a trusted retailer and e-commerce leader, and you gain the confidence of knowing that they'll receive the high-quality service and great low prices we give all our customers.

Fig. 4. Example of global affiliate reseller programme.
(See Appendix for contact details.)

Glossary of Business Terms

Ability to repay. Evidence of the wherewithal to repay any loans you arrange in connection with your enterprise.

Accommodation facility. Arrangement with (say) your Local Development Business Centre for short-term rental of desk space, secretarial services, mail handling etc.

Annual accounts. Formal statements showing the financial position of a business, which are normally drawn up by an accountant and submitted to the Inland Revenue for tax assessment purposes. They usually comprise a trading account, a profit and loss account and a balance sheet.

Assets. The total value of things owned by a business.

Attachments. Computer files that accompany the message portion of an e-mail.

Autoresponder. An electronic Internet email device which collects enquiries and which has the capability of transmitting up to seven individual responses – from immediate to follow ups.

Bizops. Universally accepted Internet jargon for business opportunities.

Book-keeping. The production of records of a business's financial transactions.

Booster grant. Local Authority Start-Up Grant (typically around £1,000).

Business administration refresher course. Local Authority crash course on business skills (normally free of charge to qualified applicants).

Business Development Executive. Your initial contact on matters relating to starting up. Based at TECs, LECs etc.

Business plan. The masterplan you prepare to convince other people that you have what it takes to run a business.

Buying signals. The telltale signs that indicate you're talking to a willing buyer.

Cash book. The accounting book which records all payments into and out of the business's bank account.

Cash flow. Controlling the flow of cash you collect from customers and other sources before you pay your suppliers and any other creditors.

Collateral. Security put up against loan arrangements, for example a house or insurance policy.

Competitive activity. Activity by your competitors in such matters as pricing, promotions, sales territory, marketing.

Contact points. Your essential personal points of contact when conducting sales negotiation. They are not always the decision makers, though.

Conversion ratios. The relationship between the number of calls you have to make to achieve a given number of confirmed sales, for example 36 calls, 12 sales. Divide 12 into 36 and the conversion ratio is 3.

Creditors. The suppliers to the business to whom money is owed and the amount owed by the business to them (contrast debtors).

Current assets. These are assets which are either cash or can be turned into cash quite quickly. They include cash, bank balances (not overdrafts), debtors, stock and work in progress. (Contrast current liabilities and fixed assets.)

Current liabilities. These are amounts owed to suppliers (creditors) together with short term loans such as bank overdrafts. Short term loans are those less than one year and so part of hire purchase liabilities may also be included under this heading where they are repayable within the next twelve months. (Contrast current assets.)

Customer base. The total number of customers with whom you are currently doing business.

Customer service. The added extras which businesses provide to ensure continued customer satisfaction, thus achieving loyalty amongst the purchasers of products and services.

Debtors. The customers of the business who owe money to the business and the amount owed. (Contrast creditors.)

Depreciation. An allowance made (charged as an expense in the profit and loss account) for the reduction in value of fixed assets, (particularly machinery, furnishings and motor vehicles) during each accounting period. See page 99 for more details.

Direct mail. Advertising and promotional material delivered to a specific and carefully targeted audience.

Discretionary funds. That amount of money you have available for paying out as you please.

Distribution channels. The patterns of distribution you have determined for your product, for example, wholesale, retail, door-to-door, direct mail.

Downlines. Those participants operating in downward levels from the sponsor in multi level marketing.

E-mail. Electronic information addressed and transmitted over the Internet.

E-mail address. Consists of a user ID, followed by an @ sign and a domain name. For example: jim@uddingston.com.

Entrepreneur. A business person who seeks to make a profit by risk and initiative.

Entrepreneurship training programme. Courses largely underwritten by government agencies, conducted by entrepreneurs in their own right and dealing exclusively with essential entrepreneurial skills.

Equity stake. Capital invested in an enterprise on a long-term or permanent basis. All or part of the share capital.

Executive summary. The concise précis of what your enterprise is all about and which appears at the very beginning of your business plan.

External capital. The amount of money (loans, grants, overdraft) you need to raise from outside sources.

Fixed assets. Items of long term use to a business such as a freehold property, fixtures and fittings.

Fixed interest rates. Those rates which are set when funding is arranged and do not vary for a given period.

Flame. An Internet message which uses profanity or otherwise belittles the recipient.

Founders' equity. The respective amounts of money each of the founding members invest in an enterprise.

Franchise. A licence for one party to set up and run a venture in a particular area for a specific period of time, using the trading name and business format of another party.

Franchisee. The party buying a franchise. (The party granting the franchise is known as a franchisor.)

Full repairing and insuring liability. A legal obligation whereby the tenant of a property is responsible for its internal and external maintenance and insurance.

Funds sourcing. Going out in the market looking for the external capital you need to get the business up and running.

Free initial training. Available in various categories (free of charge to recognised start-ups) from public sector sources.

Going concern. A well established business which appears to be trading satisfactorily (although an examination of its books and accounts may convey a different and more accurate image).

Goodwill. Sum based on the annual net profit of a business and added to its value when sold.

Gross profit. The profit derived from buying and selling goods and services, before the deduction of overheads such as rent, wages and transport costs.

Hands-on experience. Practical knowledge gained through participation as opposed to academic study.

Hidden agenda. An important and real agenda which isn't written down on any official piece of paper.

Image. The impression you give to others of yourself and your business.

Immediate catchment area. The geographical area in which you initially intend to do business.

Indigenous growth. Creating growth in the economy through encouraging locally based enterprise.

Information technology. Using computers to store and process information as opposed to entrusting it all to pen and paper.

Initial budgeting requirements. Estimating precisely how much money you will need by way of investment and sales to keep you afloat during the initial trading period.

Input tax. Value added tax charged on products and services purchased by a VAT registered trader for resale or business use.

Integrated Services Digital Network (ISDN). Currently the fastest connection capable of using existing telephone lines. ISDN enables users to connect at speeds of 128KB per second. The ISDN line is capable of transmitting voice and data simultaneously.

Intelligence gathering. The continuous gathering of information about your industry so that you always know what's happening.

Internet. A worldwide network of millions of computers and servers that uses telephone system technology to transmit information from one place to another.

Internet Service Provider (ISP). A company which provides users access to the Internet.

Jointly and severally responsible. Expression used in relation to partnerships, indicating that partners are responsible for each others' activities.

Liabilities. The money which a business owes in the forms of loans, hire purchase agreements, trade suppliers, tax etc.

Limited company. A separate legal entity which can trade in its own right. Forming limited companies can have tax advantages, and can protect the owners from paying debts if the firm runs into trouble.

Mainstream finance. Just another way of describing external finance: mainstream because it normally accounts for the bulk of the required investment.

Marketplace. Where you'll be doing business.

Marketing grants. Available only from the public sector and only to qualified start-ups for assistance with brochures, exhibition participation etc.

Marketing programme. The programme of activity that gets your business rolling.

Modem. A device that allows your computer to talk to other computers using your telephone line. Modems range in speeds of 9.6 to 33.6 KB per second.

MLM (multi level marketing). Marketing of a product or service at various levels in upward and downward directions.

Net assets. The total of **net current assets** added to **fixed assets**.

Net current assets. The sum remaining after **current liabilities** have been deducted from **current assets**.

Net profit. The profit of a business after taking account of all expenses.

Networking. Broadcasting your message to groups of people and achieving a knock-on effect in the performance of your sales programme.

New business grant. Available only from the public sector to qualified unemployed applicants with approved start-up status. Replaces Enterprise Allowance Scheme.

Output tax. Value added tax charged by a VAT registered trader on goods and services sold to customers.

Overheads. Costs incurred by a business regardless of its sales turnover.

Participating equity partner. A partner in the enterprise who has contributed to the share capital.

Partnership. A legally binding business association of two or more people. Each partner is usually equally liable for all of the partnership's debts.

Pay As You Earn (PAYE). A scheme whereby employers have to deduct tax and national insurance from employee's wages to pass them to the Inland Revenue each month.

Personal drawings. Monies taken out of a business for personal use, as noted on the balance sheet.

Personal integrity. Your personal honesty and trustworthiness. It is your most vital asset in business.

Pricing policy. The means you use to set your selling prices.

Profit and loss account. An account summarising the income and expenditure of a business for a given period and showing the surplus income (profit) or deficit (loss).

Planning permission. The legal permission which is granted by local authorities for individuals or businesses to build or change the use of premises. Planning permission may be necessary for some home-based businesses.

Professional indemnity. An insurance scheme which protects businesses against claims for problems involved in the running of the business, such as administrative errors.

Proven ideas. Business ideas that are tried, tested and seen to work in practice.

Public sector funding. Working capital obtained from the public sector by way of grants and soft loans.

Sale or return. A trading condition whereby unsold stock is returned to the supplier for a cash refund or credit against future purchases.

Scenario planning. Planning for various 'what if' situations that could occur in the future.

Schematic. A simple diagram that illustrates an idea.

Secured borrowings. Loans, overdrafts, mortgages and other financial advantages against which assets have been set by a borrower.

Security. Assets pledged by a borrower against monies borrowed, to protect the lender against defaults by the borrower.

Seed capital. The initial cash invested in a business to get it up and running.

Selling off-the-page. Getting distribution of a product or service solely by means of press advertising.

Server. Any computer that delivers (serves) information and data.

Soft loans. So called because they are arranged on very generous terms. They are available only from the public sector.

Sole trader. A self-employed individual.

Start-up. A brand new enterprise.

Stock. Finished items which are ready to be sold to customers.

Telemarketing techniques. Using the telephone (and fax) to sell direct to customers.

Template. A pattern for success, your business plan.

Trade directories. Every trade has at least one reference directory, classifying businesses according to their trading profiles.

Trading name. The name under which your enterprise will trade.

Trading out of your debts. Trying to pay off old debts by creating new business. It is normally a road to ruin.

Training & Enterprise Councils (TECs). A nationwide network of bodies set up to foster skills training and business enterprise. Operating under broad government guidelines, each regional TEC is a partnership of local public organisations and businesses, and devises its own programme of financial support and advice. See your local phone book for details.

Turnover. The total amount of money which comes into a business from all sources.

Uniform Resource Locator (URL). The standard address used to locate a Web page, Web server, or other device on the Web or on the Internet.

Unsecured loans. Loans made without any collateral.

VAT. Value Added Tax. A tax applied to a wide range of products and services, currently 17.5 per cent.

VAT threshold. The trading level at which you are obliged to register for Value Added Tax. It is currently £48,000 pa, but may be changed each year in the Chancellor's Budget.

Venture capital houses. Financial institutions you would go to first for funding if your enterprise is on a major scale.

Web site. A collection of World Wide Web documents, normally consisting of a home page and several related pages i.e. an interactive electronic book.

Working capital. The amount of money required to keep the business running effectively and solvently.

World Wide Web (WWW). The graphical segment of the Internet, which consists of millions of Web pages on servers all over the world. Each page carries an address called an URL and contains links which you click to go to other Web pages.

Youth incentive schemes. Government sponsored projects to help young unemployed persons find a job or set up in business for themselves.

Appendix 1
Training & Enterprise Councils

COMPACTs

East Midlands

Jo Sykes, Manager
Leicester Compact
Knighton Fields Teacher Centre
Herrick Road
LE2 6DH
Tel: (0116) 2448270
Fax: (0116) 2709759

Midlands

Sarah Hodskinson, EBP Manager
Liverpool Compact
The Annexe
Shorefields Comm Comp
School & Adult Education Centre
Aigburth Road
Toxteth, Liverpool
Merseyside L17 7BN
Tel: (0151) 728 9454
Fax: (0151) 728 8149

Julie Bond, Acting Director
Sefton Compact
Mast House
Off Derby Road
Bootle
Merseyside L20 7AE
Tel: (0151) 922 6822
Fax: (0151) 933 8177

South East

Heart of England Compact
c/o Heart of England TEC
26/27 The Quadrant
Abingdon Science Park
OX14 3YS
Tel: (01235) 533249
Fax: (01253) 555706

LECs

Barry McGuigan, Education
    Manager
Enterprise Ayrshire
17–19 Hill Street
Kilmarnock
Ayrshire KA3 1HA
Tel: (01563) 526623
Fax: (01563) 543636

Ian A Maclaren, Operations
    Manager
Fife Enterprise
Fast Trac
Kingdom House
Saltire Court
Glenrothes
Fife KY6 2AQ
Tel: (01592) 623152
Fax: (01592) 623199

Yvonne Brown, Operations
    Manager
Forth Valley Enterprise
Laurel House
Laurelhill Business Park
Stirling FK7 9JQ
Tel: (01786) 451919
Fax: (01786) 478123
E-mail: fveinfo@scotent.co.uk

Bruce Armitage, Director of Skills
    and Learning
Grampian Enterprise Ltd
27 Albyn Place
Aberdeen AB1 1YL
Tel: (01224) 575100
Fax: (01224) 213417

John Cunningham, Education
    Manager
Lanarkshire Development Agency
New Lanarkshire House
Strathclyde Business Park
Bells Hill
Lanarkshire ML4 3AD
Tel: (01698) 745454
Fax: (01698) 842211
E-mail: LDA@scotent.co.uk
Web site: www.lda.co.uk

Lorraine Allan, Education
**Lothian and Edinburgh Enterprise
    Ltd**
Apex House
99 Haymarket Terrace
Edinburgh EH12 5HD
Tel: (0131) 3134000
Fax: (0131) 3134231

Dave Blazk, Company Manager
Scottish Borders Careers
4 Abbotsford Rd
TD1 3DS
Tel: (01896) 754884
Fax: (01896) 758183

Skills Manager
Scottish Borders Enterprise
Bridge Street
Galasheils TD1 1SW
Tel: (01896) 758991
Fax: (01896) 758625
E-mail: frankwielbo@scotent.co.uk

Alison McNeil, Head of Skills
    Development
Argyll & The Islands Enterprise
The Enterprise Centre
Kilmory Industrial Estate
Lochgilphead
Argyll PA31 8SH
Tel: (01546) 602281
Fax: (01546) 603964

Simon Moodie, Skills
    Development Manager
Caithness & Sutherland Enterprise
Tollemache House
High Street
Thurso
Caithness KW14 8AZ
Tel: (01847) 896115
Fax: (01847) 893383

Ruth Higgs, Education Manager
Highlands & Islands Enterprise
Bridge House
20 Bridge Street
Inverness IV11 1QR
Tel: (01463) 244389
Fax: (01463) 244338

Ian Fraser, Head of Skills
    Development
Inverness & Nairn Enterprise
Castle Wynd
Inverness IV2 5DW
Tel: (01463) 713504
Fax: (01463) 712002

Morven Cameron, Education
  Manager
Lochaber Limited
St Mary's House
Gordon Square
Fort William
Inverness-shire PH33 6DY
Tel: (01397) 704326
Fax: (01397) 705309

Charles Fraser, Education
  Manager
**Moray, Badenoch & Strathspey
  Enterprise**
Elgin Business Centre
Elgin
Moray IV30 1RH
Tel: (01343) 550567
Fax: (01343) 550678

Ruth Kirkpatrick, Education
  Manager
Orkney Enterprise
14 Queen Street
Kirkwall
Orkney KW15 1JE
Tel: (01856) 874638
Fax: (01856) 872915

Anne Murray, Education Director
Ross & Cromarty Enterprise
69–71 High Street
Invergordon
Ross-shire IV18 0AA
Tel: (01349) 853666
Fax: (01349) 853833

Gordon McVie, Manager
Scottish Enterprise
120 Bothwell Street
Glasgow G2 7JP
Tel: (0141) 248 2700
Fax: (0141) 228 2319

Valerie Treneman, Manager
Shetland Enterprise
Toll Clock Shopping Centre
26 North Road
Lerwick
Shetland ZE1 0DE
Tel: (01595) 693177
Fax: (01595) 693208

Gordon Bushnell, Manager
Skye & Lochalsh Enterprise
King's House, The Green
Portree
Isle of Skye IV51 9BS
Tel: (01478) 612841
Fax: (01478) 612164

Gerry McGuigan, Manager
Western Isles Enterprise
3 Harbour View
Cromwell Street Quay
Stornoway
Isle of Lewis HS1 2DF
Tel: (01851) 703703
Fax: (01851) 704130

TECs

East

June Shimmin, Learning for Life
  Development Manager
Bedfordshire and Luton CCTE
Woburn Court, 2 Railton Road
Woburn Road Industrial Estate
Kempston
Bedfordshire MK42 7PN
Tel: (0123) 484 3100
Fax: (0123) 484 3211

Kim Norman, CEO
Business Link Cambridgeshire
Unit 2–3 Trust Court
Chivers Way, The Vision Park
Histon
Cambridge
CB4 4PW
Tel: (0122) 323 5635
Fax: (0122) 323 5631

Peter Henderson, Development
    Coordinator for Education and
    Training
Essex TEC
Redwing House
Hedgerows Business Park
Colchester Road
Chelmsford
Essex CM2 5PB
Tel: (0124) 545 0123
Fax: (0124) 545 1430

John Brittain, Education Director
Greater Peterborough CCTE
Stuart House
City Road
Peterborough PE1 1QF
Tel: (0173) 389 0808
Fax: (0173) 389 0809
E-mail: gpccte@gpccte.co.uk

Liz Wade
Greater Peterborough TEC
GPCCTE
Stuart House
City Road
Peterborough PE1 1QF
Tel: (01733) 890808
Fax: (01733) 890809

David Tofts, Education Manager
Hertfordshire TEC
45 Grosvenor Road
St Albans
Hertfordshire AL1 3AW
Tel: (0172) 781 3600
Fax: (0172) 781 3443

Manager
Norfolk and Waveney TEC
St Andrew's House
St Andrew's Street
Norwich NR2 4TP
Tel: (0160) 376 3812
Fax: (0160) 376 3813

John McCloud, Head of
    Education and Training
Suffolk TEC
2nd Floor, Crown House
Crown Street
Ipswich
Suffolk IP1 3HS
Tel: (0147) 321 8951
Fax: (0147) 323 1776

East Midlands

Joanna Irons, Head of Education
    and Training
Greater Nottingham TEC
Marina Road, Castle Marina Park
Nottingham
Nottinghamshire NG7 1TN
Tel: (0115) 941 3313
Fax: (0115) 948 4589

Sue O'Hara, Senior Education
    Manager
Leicestershire TEC
Meridian East
Meridian Business Park
Leicester LE3 2WZ
Tel: (0116) 265 1515
Fax: (0116) 265 1501

Elaine Lilley, Education Business
    Advisor
Lincolnshire TEC
Beech House, Witham Park
Waterside South
Lincoln
Lincolnshire LN5 7JH
Tel: (0152) 256 7765
Fax: (0152) 251 0534

Peter Jessop, Education and
    Training Manager
North Derbyshire TEC
Block C, St Mary's Court
St Mary's Gate
Chesterfield S41 7TD
Tel: (0124) 66551158/0976 432 311
Fax: (0124) 623 8489

Terry Phillips, Education and
  Training Manager
North Nottinghamshire TEC
Centre for Business Excellence
Edwinstowe House
Edwinstowe
Nottinghamshire NG21 9PR
Tel: (0162) 382 4624
Fax: (0162) 382 4070

Neville Royan, Education
  Manager
Northamptonshire CCTE
Royal Pavillion
Summerhouse Road
Moulton Park Industrial Estate
Northampton NN3 6BJ
Tel: (0160) 467 1200
Fax: (0160) 467 0362

Rachel Hatchet, Education Liaison
Southern Derbyshire CCTE
St Helen's Court
St Helen's Street
Derby
Derbyshire DE1 3GY
Tel: (0133) 229 0550
Fax: (0133) 229 2188

London

Colin Ainsworth, Education
  Manager
AZTEC
Manorgate House
2 Manorgate Road
Kingston-upon-Thames KT2 7AL
Tel: (020) 8547 3934
Fax: (020) 8547 3884

Andy Miller, Head of Schools
Focus Central London
Centre Point
103 New Oxford Street
London WC1A 1DR
Tel: (020) 7896 8484
Fax: (020) 7896 8686

Fiona Paterson, Education and
  Lifelong Learning
LETEC (London East TEC)
Boardman House, 64 Broadway
Stratford
London E15 4EA
Tel: (020) 8432 0000
Fax: (020) 8432 0399

Barbara Atkinson, Education
  Manager
North London TEC
Dumayne House
1 Fox Lane
Palmers Green
London N13 4AB
Tel: (020) 8447 9422
Fax: (020) 8882 5931

Linda Davies, Education and
  Business Partnership Manager
North West London TEC
Kirkfield House
118–120 Station Road
Harrow
Middlesex HA1 2RL
Tel: (020) 8901 5000
Fax: (020) 8901 5100

Virginia Waterhouse, Education
  Manager
SOLOTEC
Lancaster House
7 Elmfield Road
Bromley
Kent BR1 1LT
Tel: (020) 8313 9232
Fax: (020) 8313 9245

Laurie South, Education Business
  Manager
West London TEC
West London Centre
15–21 Staines Road
Hounslow
Middlesex TW3 3HA
Tel: (020) 8577 1010
Fax: (020) 8570 9969

Merseyside

Merseyside TEC
Tithebarn House
Tithebarn Street
Liverpool L2 2NZ
Tel: (0151) 236 0026
Fax: (0151) 236 4013

Ann Mabbott, Education Manager
St Helens CCTE
St Helens Technology Campus
St Helens
Merseyside WA9 1UB
Tel: (0174) 474 2000
Fax: (0174) 474 2040

North East

David Lane, Senior Education
    Manager
County Durham TEC
Horndale Avenue
Aycliffe Industrial Park
Newton Aycliffe
County Durham DL5 6XS
Tel: (0191) 374 4000
Fax: (0191) 374 4010

Alan Taylorson, Education
    Manager
Sunderland City TEC Ltd
Business and Innovation Centre
Sunderland Enterprise Park
Wearfield
Sunderland SR5 2TA
Tel: (0191) 516 6000
Fax: (0191) 516 6161
E-mail: alan.taylorson
    @sunderland.tec.org.uk

Lee Chapman, Careers Advisor
Tees Valley TEC
Training & Enterprise House
2 Queen's Square
Middlesborough TS2 1AA
Tel: (0164) 223 1023
Fax: (0164) 223 2480

Alan Wallace, District Manager
Tees Valley TEC
Stratford House
Ramsgate
Stockton on Tees TS18 1BT
Tel: (01642) 616757
Fax: (01642) 612176
E-mail: awallace:teesvalleytec.co.uk

Ray Steel, Education Manager
Tyneside TEC
Moorgate House
5th Avenue Business Park
Team Valley Trading Park
Gateshead NE11 0HF
Tel: (0191) 491 6000
Fax: (0191) 491 6159

Northern Ireland

Jim McColgan, Education
    Manager
NORIBIC Ltd
Business and Innovation Centre
9 Shipquay Street
Londonderry
N. Ireland BT48 6DJ
Tel: (028) 7126 4242
Fax: (028) 7126 9025

Northwest

Norman Garner, Education
    Manager
Bolton Bury TEC
Clive House
Clive Street
Bolton BL1 1ET
Tel: (0120) 439 7350
Fax: (0120) 436 3212

Clive Wilkinson, Education
    Manager
CEWTEC
Egerton House, 2 Tower Road
Birkenhead
Wirral L41 1FN
Tel: (0151) 650 0555
Fax: (0151) 650 0777

John Jordan, Education Manager
ELTEC
Red Rose Court
Clayton Business Park
Clayton le Moors
Accrington
Lancashire BB5 5JR
Tel: (0125) 430 1333
Fax: (0125) 439 9090
E-mail: elebp@compnet.co.uk

Barbara Cannon, Education
  Manager
Enterprise Cumbria
Venture House
Guard Street
Workington CA14 4EW
Tel: (0190) 066 9911
Fax: (0190) 060 4027

Viv King, Education Manager
LAWTEC
Taylor House
Caxton Road
Fulwood
Preston PR2 9ZB
Tel: (0177) 279 2111
Fax: (0177) 279 2777

Mich Noque, Education Manager
Manchester TEC
Lee House
90 Great Bridgewater Street
Manchester M1 5JW
Tel: (0161) 236 7222
Fax: (0161) 236 8878

Linda Bloomfield, CEO
Merseyside TEC
Tithebarn House
Tithebarn Street
Liverpool L2 2NZ
Tel: (0151) 236 0026
Fax: (0151) 236 4013

Jane Dickens, Education Manager
North & Mid Cheshire TEC
Spencer House
Dewhurst Road
Birchwood
Warrington WA3 7PP
Tel: (0192) 582 6515
Fax: (0192) 582 0215

John Gracie, CEO
Oldham CCTE
Meridian Centre
King Street
Oldham OL8 1EZ
Tel: (0161) 620 0006
Fax: (0161) 620 0030

Cliff Ellison, CEO
Rochdale Borough CCTE
St James Place
160–162 Yorkshire Street
Rochdale
Lancashire OL16 2DL
Tel: (0170) 664 4909
Fax: (0170) 664 9979

Liz Davis, CEO
South & East Cheshire TEC
PO Box 37
Middlewich Industrial & Business
  Park
Dalton Way
Middlewich
Cheshire CW10 0HU
Tel: (0160) 673 7009
Fax: (0160) 673 7022

John Fox, Director of Education
  and Training
Stockport & High Peak TEC
1 St Peters Square
Stockport SK1 1NN
Tel: (0161) 477 8830
Fax: (0161) 480 7243

Clive Moss, General Advisor
Wigan CCTE
The Investment Centre
Waterside Drive
Wigan WN3 5BA
Tel: (0194) 270 5705
Fax: (0194) 270 5272

Peter Hulmes, CEO
NW Merseyside St Helens CCTE
St Helens Technology Campus
St Helens
Merseyside WA9 1UB
Tel: (0174) 474 2000
Fax: (0174) 474 2040

South East

Elaine Crosthwaite, Education
   Manager
Hampshire TEC
25 Thackeray Mall
Fareham PO16 0PQ
Tel: (0132) 923 0099
Fax: (0132) 923 7733

Carol Brand, Education Manager
Heart of England TEC
26–27 The Quadrant
Abingdon Science Park
Abingdon OX14 3YS
Tel: (0123) 555 3249
Fax: (0123) 555 5706

Nicky Wichlow
Skills and Learning
Kent TEC
26 Kings Hill Avenue
Kings Hill
West Malling ME19 4TA
Tel: (0173) 222 0000
Fax: (0173) 284 1641

Mike Mason, Education Business
   Partnership Co-ordinator
**Milton Keynes & North Bucks
   CCTE**
Tempus
249 Midsummer Boulevard
Central Milton Keynes MK9 1EU
Tel: (0190) 825 9000
Fax: (0190) 823 0130
E-mail: tempus@mk-chamber.co.uk
Web site: www.mk-chamber.co.uk

Geoff Marshall, Education
   Manager
Surrey TEC
Technology House
48–54 Goldsworth Road
Woking
Surrey GU21 1LE
Tel: (0148) 372 8190
Fax: (0148) 375 5259

Geoff Gilvear, Education Manager
Sussex Enterprise
Greenacre Court, Station Road
Burgess Hill
West Sussex RH15 9DS
Tel: (0144) 425 9259
Fax: (0144) 425 9190

Susan Jones
Director of Education
Thames Valley Enterprise
Pacific House, Imperial Way
Reading
RG2 0TF
Tel: (0118) 921 4000
Fax: (0118) 975 3054

Diane Perry-Yates, Education
   Manager
Wight TEC
Mill Court
Furrlongs
Newport
Isle of Wight PO30 2AA
Tel: (0198) 382 2818
Fax: (0198) 352 7063

South West

Carol Mullard, Education
  Manager
Dorset TEC
25 Oxford Road
Bournemouth BH8 8EY
Tel: (0120) 246 6400
Fax: (0120) 229 9457

Sandra Thomas, Education
  Manager
Gloucestershire TEC
Conway House
33–35 Worcester Street
Gloucester GL1 3AJ
Tel: (0145) 252 4488
Fax: (0145) 250 9537

Chris Roberts, Education Manager
Prosper (Devon & Cornwall TEC)
Prosper House
Brooklands
Budshead Road
Crownhill
Plymouth PL6 5XR
Tel: (0175) 278 5785
Fax: (0175) 277 0925

Martin Alliston, Education
  Manager
Somerset TEC
East Reach House
East Reach
Taunton TA1 3EN
Tel: (0182) 332 1188
Fax: (0182) 325 6174

Bill Adshead, Head of Training
Western TEC (WESTEC)
St Lawrence House
29–31 Broad Street
Bristol BS99 7HR
Tel: (0117) 927 7116
Fax: (0117) 922 6664

Norman Atkin, Education
  Manager
Wiltshire & Swindon TEC
The Bora Building
Westlea Campus
Westlea Down
Swindon SN5 7EZ
Tel: (0179) 351 3644
Fax: (0179) 350 1555

Wales

Anthony Drew, CEO
CELTEC – North Wales TEC
St Asaph Business Park
St Asaph
Denbighshire LL17 0JL
Tel: (0174) 553 8500
Fax: (0174) 558 5444

Allen Williams, CEO
Mid Glamorgan TEC
Unit 17–20 Centre Court
Main Avenue
Treforest Industrial Estate
Pontypridd
Mid Glamorgan CF37 5LY
Tel: (0144) 384 1594
Fax: (0144) 384 1578

Paul Sheldon, CEO
South Glamorgan TEC
2–7 Drake Walk
Brigantine Place
Atlantic Wharf
Cardiff CF1 5AN
Tel: (029) 2022 61000
Fax: (029) 2024 50424

Chris Jones, CEO
West Wales TEC
Orchard House
Orchard Street
Swansea
West Glamorgan SA1 5DJ
Tel: (0179) 246 0355
Fax: (0179) 235 4701

West Midlands

Mike Bells, Head of Education
Birmingham TEC Limited
Chaplin Court
80 Hurst Street
Birmingham B5 4TG
Tel: (0121) 6224419
Fax: (0121) 6221600

Rachel Lewis-Bell, Head of
  Education
Coventry and Warwickshire CCTE
Oak Tree Court
Binley Business Park
Harry Weston Road
Coventry CV3 2LN
Tel: (024) 7636 54321
Fax: (024) 7634 50242

Dudley Light, Education Manager
Dudley TEC
3 Dudley Court South
Waterfront East, Level Street
Brierley Hill
Dudley DY5 1XN
Tel: (01384) 485000
Fax: (01384) 483399

Val Monaghan, Manager
**Herefordshire & Worcestershire
  CCTE**
Placement Service
Pitmaston House, Malvern Rd
Worcester WR2 4Z9
Tel: (01905) 42 5000
Fax: (01905) 429 108
Web site: www.worcestershire.gov.uk

Michael Kilduff, Head of
  Education and Training
Sandwell TEC
1st Floor
Black Country House
Rounds Green Road
Oldbury B69 2DG
Tel: (0121) 543 2222
Fax: (0121) 543 4444

Angela Robinson, CEO
Shropshire CCTE
Trevithick House
Stafford Park 4
Telford TF3 3BA
Tel: (0195) 220 8200
Fax: (0195) 220 8208

Chris Washington
Education
Staffordshire TEC
Festival Way
Festival Park
Stoke on Trent ST1 5TQ
Tel: (01782) 202733
Fax: (01782) 286215

Carl Mason, Education Manager
Walsall TEC
5th Floor
Townend House
Townend Square
Walsall WS1 1NS
Tel: (0192) 242 4242
Fax: (0192) 242 4243

Julie James, Education Manager
Wolverhampton CCTE
Pendeford Business Park
Wobaston Road
Wolverhampton WV9 5HA
Tel: (0190) 244 5500
Fax: (0190) 244 5200

Yorkshire & Humberside

David Wilkinson, CEO
Bradford & District TEC
Mercury House
4 Manchester Road
Bradford BD5 0QL
Tel: (0127) 475 1333
Fax: (0127) 475 1344

Roger Grasby, CEO
North Yorkshire TEC
TEC House
7 Pioneer Business Park
Amy Johnson Way
Clifton Moorgate
York YO3 8TN
Tel: (0190) 469 1939
Fax: (0191) 469 0411

Hilary Bennett, Education
  Manager
Calderdale and Kirklees TEC
Park View House
Woodvale Office Park
Woodvale Road
Brighouse HD6 4AB
Tel: (0148) 440 0770
Fax: (0148) 440 0672

Education Manager
Humberside TEC
The Maltings
Silvester Square
Silvester Street
Hull HU1 3HL
Tel: (0148) 222 6491
Fax: (0148) 221 3206

Barry Blanchard, Education
  Manager
Leeds TEC
Belgrave Hall
Belgrave Street
Leeds LS2 8DD
Tel: (0113) 234 7666
Fax: (0113) 243 8126

Sean Withers, Education Advisor
North Yorkshire TEC
TEC House
7 Pioneer Business Park
Amy Johnson Way
York YO30 4TN
Tel: (0190) 469 1939
Fax: (0190) 469 0411

Graham Fisher, Contracts
  Education Development
  Manager.
Rotherham CCTE
Moorgate House
Moorgate Road
Rotherham S60 2EN
Tel: (0170) 983 0511
Fax: (0170) 936 2519

Ian Barlow, Education Manager
Sheffield TEC
St Mary's Court
55 St Mary's Road
Sheffield S2 4AQ
Tel: (0114) 270 1911
Fax: (0114) 275 2634

Catherine Lunn, Education
  Manager
Wakefield TEC
Grove Hall
60 College Grove Road
Wakefield WF1 3RN
Tel: (0192) 429 9907
Fax: (0192) 420 1837

East

Jeff Offer, EBP Director
Bedfordshire Partnership
Maryland College
Leighton Street
Woburn
Milton Keynes
Bedfordshire MK17 9JD
Tel: (01525) 290725
Fax: (01525) 292940

Linda Gaze, BEP Manager
BEP South East Essex (BEPSEE)
c/o Essex Careers & Business
  Partnership
Burley House
15 High Street
Rayleigh
Essex SS6 7EW
Tel: (01268) 749600

Maureen Gow
Cambs TEC
Unit 2–3 Trust Court
Chivers Way
The Vision park
Histon CB4 4PW
Tel: (01223) 235635
Fax: (01223) 235631

Liz Wade
Greater Peterborough TEC
GPCCTE
Stuart House
City Road
Peterborough PE1 1QF
Tel: (01733) 890808
Fax: (01733) 890809

Gloria Sayer, EBP Manager
Hertfordshire EBP
Hertfordshire TEC
45 Grosvenor Road
St Albans
Hertfordshire AL1 3AW
Tel: (01727) 813566/7
Fax: (01727) 813560
E-mail: gloria.sayer@herts.tec.co.uk

Marilyn Hopkins, BEP Manager
Mid Essex BEP
c/o Essex Training Ltd
Farrow Road
Widford Industrial Estate
Chelmsford
Essex CM1 3TH
Tel: (01245) 268590
Fax: (01245) 494261

Yvonne Barclay, EBP Manager
Norfolk EBP
Professional Development Centre
Woodside Road
Norwich
East Anglia NR7 9QL
Tel: (01603) 433276
Fax: (01603) 700693

Pam Osbourne, BEP Manager
North East Essex BEP
c/o Chamber of Commerce
8–9 St Peters Court
Middleborough
Colchester
Essex CO1 1WD
Tel: (01206) 762888
Fax: (01206) 502506

Mike Williamson, BEP Manager
South West Essex BEP
c/o Chalvedon School
Wickford Avenue
Pitsea
Basildon
Essex SS13 3HL
Tel: (01268) 552536 Ext 235
Fax: (01268) 551209
E-mail: bonus@swebep.demon.
    co.uk

Lorraine Marchant, EBP Manager
Suffolk Partnership Ltd
2nd Floor
Crown House
Crown Street
Ipswich IP1 3HS
Tel: (01473) 296089
Fax: (01473) 231776

Rachel Foulger, EBP Manager
Waveney EBP
Northern Area Education Office
Adrian House
Alexandra Road
Lowestoft
Suffolk NR32 1PL
Tel: (01502) 405214
Fax: (01502) 405222

Robert Gray, BEP Manager
West Essex BEP & Compact
Malting Mead
Mill Lane
Churchgate Street
Old Harlow
Essex CM17 0LN
Tel: (01279) 453933
Fax: (01279) 453933
E-mail: 101771.2300@compuserve.
com.

East Midlands

Gillian Harding, Education
    Manager
Greater Nottingham EBP
Marina Road
Castle Marina Park
Nottingham
Nottinghamshire NG7 1TN
Tel: (0115) 941 3313
Fax: (0115) 948 4589
E-mail: GHarding@gntec.co.uk

Barbara Chantrill, EBP Manager/
    Director
Leicestershire EBP
c/o Leicestershire TEC
Meridian East
Meridian Business Park
Leicester
Leicestershire LE3 2WZ
Tel: (0116) 2651619
Fax: (0116) 2651678
E-mail: admin@leicsebp.telme.com

Elaine Lilley, Education Business
    Advisor
Lincolnshire TEC
Beech House
Witham Park
Waterside South
Lincoln
Lincolnshire LN5 7JH
Tel: (0152) 256 7765
Fax: (0152) 251 0534

John O'Callaghan, EBP Manager
North Derbyshire Partnership
Careers Service
61–63 Low Pavement
Chesterfield
Derbyshire S40 1PB
Tel: (01246) 557847
Fax: (01246) 297626

Richard Kirkland, EBP Manager
North Nottinghamshire EBP
    North Nottinghamshire TEC
    Ltd
Edwinstowe House
High Street
Edwinstowe
Mansfield
Nottinghamshire NG21 9PR
Tel: (01623) 827984
Fax: (01623) 825413
E-mail: enquiries@nntec.demon.
    co.uk

Neville Royan, EBP Manager
Northamptonshire Chamber of
    Commerce
Training and Enterprise
Royal Pavillion
Summerhouse Road
Moulton Park Industrial Estate
Northampton
Northamptonshire NN3 6BJ
Tel: (01604) 671200
Fax: (01604) 670362

London

James Keating, Manager
Barking and Dagenham EBP
4th Floor
Roycraft House
15 Linton Road
Barking
Essex IG11 8JB
Tel: (020) 8270 6623
Fax: (020) 8270 4978

Sue Read, EBP Manager
Barnet EBP
Manorside CDC
Squires Lane, Church End
Finchley N3 2AB
Tel: (020) 8349 2793
Fax: (020) 8346 5458

Brenda Parsons, EBP Manager
Bexley EBP
Hill View
Hill View Drive
Welling
Kent DA16 3RY
Tel: (020) 8303 7777 x434
Fax: (020) 8319 4302
E-mail: bexleyebp@solotec.edex.
co.uk

Mike Barnes, EBP Manager
Bromley EBP
Education Development Centre
Church Lane
Princes Plain
Bromley
Kent BR2 8LD
Tel: (020) 8462 5046
Fax: (020) 8462 7786
E-mail: ebp@etsd.edex.co.uk

Helen Jones, Education
Development Officer
**Business & Education Succeeding
Together**
Professional Centre
Franciscan Road
Tooting
London SW17 8HE
Tel: (020) 8682 3767
Fax: (020) 8682 0740

Bob Page, EBP Manager
Camden EBP
Medburn Centre
136 Chalton Street
London NW1 1RX
Tel: (020) 7387 1995
Fax: (020) 7383 0875

Tony Slonecki, EBP Manager
Croydon EBP
1 Wandle Road
Croydon
Surrey CR9 1HY
Tel: (020) 8395 3311
Fax: (020) 8395 3202

David Scott, EBP Manager
Ealing EBP
Acton Town Hall
Winchester Street
London W3 6NE
Tel: (020) 8832 6234
Fax: (020) 8832 6236

Peter O'Brien, EBP Manager
Enfield EBP
Enfield Business Centre
201 Hertford Road
Enfield EN3 5JH
Tel: (020) 8443 2114
Fax: (020) 8443 3822
E-mail: enfield.ebp@dial.pipex.com

Dave Newson, EBP Manager
Greenwich EBP
c/o Kidbrooke School
Corelli Road
London SE3 8EP
Tel: (020) 8319 0610
Fax: (020) 8319 3042
E-mail: davenewson@
greenwich-ebp.org.uk

Faith Muir, EBP Manager
Hackney EBP
Edith Cavell Building
Enfield Road
London N1 5BA
Tel: (020) 8356 7434
Fax: (020) 356 7343

Jake Scott, EBP Manager
**Hammersmith and Fulham Satellite
EBP**
c/o Education Department
Cambridge House
Cambridge Grove
London W6 0LE
Tel: (020) 8576 5635
Fax: (020) 8600 4982
E-mail: jakemerri@msn.com

Roy Stewart, EBP Manager
Haringey EBP
Unit 1A
Lee Valley Technopark
Ashley Road
Tottenham
London N17 9LN
Tel: (020) 8880 4460
Fax: (020) 8880 4479
E-mail: haringey.ebp@hebp.co.uk
Web site: www.hebp.co.uk

Dave Butler, Manager
Havering EBP
c/o HHCS
Settle Road
Harold Hill
Romford RM3 9XR
Tel: (01708) 378378
Fax: (01708) 378123

Maureen Jackson, Manager
Hillingdon EBP
TVEI Curriculum Development
 Unit
Express Dairy Ltd
430 Victoria Road
South Ruislip HA4 0HP
Tel: (020) 8841 4224
Fax: (020) 8841 4314
E-mail: mpjackson@lbhill.gov.uk

Hugh Magee, EBP Manager
Hounslow EBP
Education Department
The Civic Centre
Lampton Road
Hounslow
Middlesex TW3 4DN
Tel: (020) 8862 5702
Fax: (020) 8862 5708
E-mail: hugh.magee@education.
 hounslow.gov.uk

Kay Chaffer, EBP Manager
Islington EBP
Barnsbury Centre
Offord Road
London N1 1QF
Tel: (020) 7457 5789
Fax: (020) 7457 5500

Gillian Morris, Chief Executive
Merton EBP
c/o Phoenix College
Central Road
Morden
Surrey SM4 5SE
Tel: (020) 8255 2431
Fax: (020) 8255 2432
E-mail: info@mebp.org.uk
Web site: www.mebp.org.uk

Nairn Norman, EBP Director
Newham EBP
Broadway House
322 High Street
Stratford
London E15 1AJ
Tel: (020) 8557 8734
Fax: (020) 8503 0654
E-mail: newham.ebp@newham.
 gov.uk

Linda Davies, EBP Manager
North West London EBP
Kirkfield House
118–120 Station Road
Harrow
Middlesex HA1 2RL
Tel: (020) 8424 8866
Fax: (020) 8901 5100
E-mail: linda.davies@nwltec.co.uk

Terry Higgins, EBP Manager
Redbridge BEP
Taste Building Teachers Centre
Melbourne Road
Ilford
Essex IG1 4HT
Tel: (020) 8514 1100
Fax: (020) 8553 2641

James Trolland, EBP Manager
Richmond EBP
c/o The Stag Brewery Company
Lower Richmond Road
London SW14 7ET
Tel: (020) 8876 3434
Fax: (020) 8392 5549

Maggie Waller, Schools Officers/
EBP
Richmond on Thames EBP
London Borough of Richmond on
Thames
Education Department
Regal House, London Road
Twickenham TW1 3QB
Tel: (020) 8891 7508
Fax: (020) 8891 7714

Carol Kay, Education Business
Adviser
Southwark EBA
Southwark Teaching Resource
Centre
Cator Street
London SE15 6AA
Tel: (020) 7525 2828
Fax: (020) 7525 2825
E-mail: yfs61@dial.pipex.com

Ian Smith, EBP Manager
Sutton EBP
Education Department
The Grove
Carshalton SM5 3AL
Tel: (020) 8770 6519
Fax: (020) 8770 6545

Mike Tyler, EBP Manager
Tower Hamlets EBP
Sunley House, Toynbee Hall Site
28 Commercial Street
London E1 6LS
Tel: (020) 7377 9497
Fax: (020) 7375 2323
E-mail: tylerm@thebp.demon.co.uk

Peter Waller, EBP Director
Waltham Forest EBP
Education Centre, Queens Road
Walthamstow
London E17 8QS
Tel: (020) 8521 3311
Fax: (020) 8509 9668

Nigel Massey
Community Partnerships
Westminster Learning Partnership
13th Floor, Westminster City Hall
64 Victoria Street
London SW1E 6QP
Tel: (020) 7641 3000
Fax: (020) 7641 3404
E-mail: nmassey@westminster.gov.uk
Web site: www.westminster.gov.uk

Merseyside

Andy Page
Partnership Development
Career Connections Ltd
The Partnership Centre
Dock Street
Ellesmere Port
South Wirral
Merseyside L65 4DH
Tel: (0151) 356 9244/55/56
Fax: (0151) 356 9277

Dave Morgan, EBP Manager
Knowsley Compact and EBP
35 Wilson Road
Huyton Industrial Estate
Huyton
Knowsley
Merseyside L36 6AE
Tel: (0151) 477 0079
Fax: (0151) 477 0090
E-mail: dave@knowsley-
compact.dem

Michael McCann
Merseyside EBP
c/o Merseyside TEC
Tithebarn House
Liverpool L2 2NZ
Tel: (0151) 236 0026
Fax: (0151) 236 4013

Phil Robson, Employer
Partnership Manager
St Helens EBP
SmithKline Beecham Building
Westfield Street
St Helens
Merseyside WA10 1QQ
Tel: (01744) 633500
Fax: (01744) 633501
E-mail: ebp@sthelenscareers.
prestel.co.uk
Web site: www.merseyworld.
com/sthelens_careers

North East

Jane Ritchie, EBP Manager
**Durham Business & Education
Executive**
Broom Cottages Primary School
Ferryhill
Co Durham DL17 8AN
Tel: (01740) 652681
Fax: (01740) 657005
E-mail: dbee@durham.gov.uk

Harry Ridley, EBP Manager
Gateshead EBP
Dryden Professional Development
Centre
Evistones Road
Gateshead NE9 5UR
Tel: (0191) 4824133
Fax: (0191) 4826500
E-mail: h.ridley@education.
gatesheadmbc.gov.uk

Eunice Roberts, EBP Manager
Newcastle EBP
Pendower Hall
West Road
Newcastle upon Tyne NE15 6PP
Tel: (0191) 2744444
Fax: (0191) 2748690

Paul Reynolds, Partnership
Director
North Tyneside EBP
EBP Centre
Linskill Centre
Linskill Terrace
North Shields
Tyne and Wear NE30 2BD
Tel: (0191) 2005878
Fax: (0191) 2005885
E-mail: ntebp@rmplc.co.uk

Norman Tomlin/Louise Woodman
Education Business
Co-ordinators
Northumberland TEC
2 Craster Court
Manor Walks
Cramlington
Northumberland NE23 6XX
Tel: (01670) 713303
Fax: (01670) 713323
E-mail: norman_tomlin@ntec.
co.uk
E-mail: louise_woodman@ntec.
co.uk
Web site: www.zebra.co.uk/ntec/

Margaret Frostick, EBP Director
South Tyneside EBP
Chuter Ede Education Centre
Galsworthy Road
South Shields, Tyne & Wear
Northumberland NE34 9UG
Tel: (0191) 5191909

Alan Taylorson, Education Manager
Sunderland City TEC Ltd
Business and Innovation Centre
Sunderland Enterprise Park
Wearfield
Sunderland SR5 2TA
Tel: (0191) 516 6000
Fax: (0191) 516 6161
E-mail: alan.taylorson@
    sunderland.tec.org.uk

Alan Wallace, District Manager
Tees Valley TEC
Stratford House
Ramsgate
Stockton on Tees TS18 1BT
Tel: (01642) 616757
Fax: (01642) 612176
E-mail: awallace@teesvalleytec.co.uk

Northern Ireland

Ken Lindsay, Chairman
**Antrim Business Education
    Partnership**
c/o W&G Baird Ltd
Greystone Press
Antrim BT41 2RS
Tel: (028) 9446 3911
Fax: (028) 9446 6250

Brendan Vallely, Chairperson
**Armagh Business Education
    Partnership**
c/o J F McKenna
66 Cathedral Road
Armagh
Co Armagh
Tel: (028) 3752 4800
Fax: (028) 3752 2227

Colin McIlwaine
Ballycastle/Ballymoney BEP
c/o The Kendall Company
20 Garrydoff Road
Ballymoney
Co Antrim BT53 7AP
Tel: (028) 2766 2324
Fax: (028) 2766 4799

Ian McAvoy, Chairman
**Ballymena Business Education
    Partnership**
c/o Magee Clothing
11–17 Paradise Avenue
Ballymena BT42 3EA
Tel: (028) 2564 6211
Fax: (028) 2564 5111

Harry Shannon, Chairman
Banbridge BEP
c/o Banbridge High School
Primrose Gardens
Banbridge
Co Down BT32 3EP
Tel: (028) 4062 2471
Fax: (028) 4062 8280

Michael McFaul, Chairman
**Carrickfergus Area Business Links
    with Education**
c/o Carrickfergus Library
Joymount Court
Carrickfergus
Co Antrim BT38 7DQ
Tel: (028) 9336 2261
Fax: (028) 9336 0589

William Montgomery, Chairman
Coleraine BEP
c/o BKS
47 Ballycairn Road
Coleraine
Co Londonderry BT51 3HZ
Tel: (028) 7035 2311
Fax: (028) 8035 7637
E-mail: wmontgomery@bks.co.uk

Sam Dowds, Chairman
**Craigavon Business Education
Partnership**
c/o Ulster Carpet Mills
Castle Island Factory
Garvaghy Road
Portadown
Tel: (028) 3839 5128
Fax: (028) 3833 3142

Martina Campbell, Secretary
**Dungannon & Cookstown Business
Education Partnership**
Unit 45 B Dungannon Enterprise
Centre
2 Coalisland Road
Dungannon BT71 6JY
Tel: (028) 8775 3854
Fax: (028) 8772 7704

Owen Fyfe
East Antrim Industry Links
c/o Larne Business Centre
Unit 10/11
Larne
Co Antrim BT40 3AW
Tel: (028) 2827 3337
Fax: (028) 2827 4932

Christine Magowan
Education
East Belfast/Castereagh BEP
c/o European Components Co Ltd
770 Upper Newtownards Road
Belfast BT16 0UL
Tel: (028) 9055 7200
Fax: (028) 9055 7300

Kenny Maguire, Secretary
**Fermanagh Education Industry
Group**
c/o Training and Employment
Agency
Paget Square
Enniskillen
Co Fermanagh BT74 7HS
Tel: (028) 6632 3511
Fax: (028) 6632 6122

Jim McColgan, Chairman
**Foyle Business Education
Partnership**
c/o NORIBIC
9 Shipquay Street
Londonderry BT84 6DJ
Tel: (028) 7126 4242
Fax: (028) 7126 9025

Linda McGuiness
Limavady & Dungiven BEP
Roe Valley Enterprise Centre
Aghanloo Industrial Estate
Limavady
Co Londonderry BT49 0HE
Tel: (028) 7777 62323
Fax: (028) 7777 65707

Robert G Millar, Chairman
**Lisburn Industry Education Liaison
Group**
c/o Millar & Sons
Lisburn BT27 4SP
Tel: (028) 9266 3318
Fax: (028) 9267 6766

Chris McCarney, Chairman
**Magherafelt Area Business
Education Partnership**
Magherafelt District Council
50 Ballyronan
Ballyronan Road
Magherafelt
Co Londonderry BT45 E10
Tel: (028) 7963 2151
Fax: (028) 7963 1240

Brian Mackey, Chairperson
Newry & Mourne BEP
c/o Adria Ltd
Carnabrie Industrial Estate
Newry
Co Down BT35 6QJ
Tel: (028) 3025 4400
Fax: (028) 3026 7359

Jim McCurdy, Chairman
Newtownabbey BEP
c/o Monkstown Community
    School
Bridge Road
Monkstown
Newtonabbey BT37 0EG
Tel: (028) 9086 7431
Fax: (028) 9071 6828

Sadie Bergin, Development
    Manager
Western Region NIBEP
c/o Business in the Community
Chamber of Commerce House
1 St Columb's Court
Bishop Street
Londonderry BT48 6PT
Tel: (028) 7136 5786
Fax: (028) 7137 4683

Pauline Donnelly, Development
    Manager
Southern Region NIBEP
c/o Business in the Community
Banbridge Enterprise Centre
Scarva Road Industrial Estate
Banbridge BT23 3QD
Tel: (028) 4062 5892
Fax: (028) 4062 2264

Trevor Greenwood, Chairman
**North Belfast Business Education
    Partnership**
c/o Belfast Model School for Girls
Dunkeld Gardens
Belfast BT14 6NT
Tel: (028) 9039 1768
Fax: (028) 9071 6828

Dominic McCullough, Chairman
**North Downs & Ards Business
    Education Partnership**
c/o T&EA
High Street
Bangor, Co Down
Tel: (028) 9127 9999
Fax: (028) 9146 5747

Louise McLean, Development
    Manager
**Northern Ireland BEP Business in
    the Community**
c/o European Components
770 Upper Newtownards Road
Belfast BT16 0UL
Tel: (028) 9041 0410
Fax: (028) 9041 9030

Jim Caves, Regional Education
    Manager
Northern Ireland BEP (NIBEP)
c/o Business in the Community
c/o BP Oil UK Ltd
Airport Road West
Belfast BT3 9EA
Tel: (028) 9041 0410
Fax: (028) 9041 9030

Michael McAleer, Chairman
**Omagh Education Industry Liaison
    Group**
c/o Training and Employment
    Agency
Kevlin Buildings
Kevlin Avenue
Omagh BT78 1ER
Tel: (028) 8225 5500
Fax: (028) 8225 5511

Dan Corr, Chairperson
South/West Belfast BEP
c/o Nationwide Building Society
53 Royal Avenue
Belfast BT1 1LX
Tel: (028) 9088 0252
Fax: (028) 9088 0256

Karen Tarr, Chairman
**Strabane Education Industry
    Liaison Group**
c/o Adria Ltd
Beechmount Avenue
Strabane
Co Tyrone BT82 9BG
Tel: (028) 7138 2568
Fax: (028) 7138 2910

North West

Neil Mawdsley
Blackburn & Darwen EDP
(serviced by East Lancs)
GEC Clayton Business Park
Clayton le Moors BB5 5JW
Tel: (01254) 389898
Fax: (01254) 239084

Bob Dawson, EBP Manager
Bolton Bury EBP
Bolton Bury TEC
Clive House
Clive Street
Bolton BL1 1ET
Tel: (01204) 374634
Fax: (01204) 336335
E-mail: ssharrock@bolton-and-
bury-chamber.co.uk

Neil Mawdsley
Burnley EDP (serviced by East
Lancs)
GEC Clayton Business Park
Clayton le Moors BB5 5JW
Tel: (01254) 389898

Linda Smye, EBP Manager
Carlisle EBP
Venture House
Guard Street
Workington
Cumbria CA14 4EW
Tel: (01900) 66991
Fax: (01900) 604027

Mike Higgins, Development
Manager
Central Lancashire EBP Ltd
Partnership Link
Croston House
Lancashire Enterprises Business
Park
Centurion Way
Leyland PR5 1TZ
Tel: (01772) 622030
Fax: (01772) 622656

David Barber, Development
Manager
EBP (West Lancashire) Ltd
Partnership Link
Croston House
Lancashire Enterprises Business
Park, Centurion Way
Leyland PR5 1TZ
Tel: (01772) 622030
Fax: (01722) 622656

Linda Smye, EBP Manager
Eden EBP
Venture House, Guard Street
Workington
Cumbria CA14 4EW
Tel: (01900) 66991
Fax: (01900) 604027

John Jordan, Education Manager
ELTEC
Red Rose Court
Clayton Business Park
Clayton le Moors, Accrington
Lancashire BB5 5JR
Tel: (0125) 430 1333
Fax: (0125) 439 9090
E-mail: elebp@compnet.co.uk

Tony Gill, EBP Project Manager
Furness EBP
Lake District Business Park
Mint Bridge Road
Kendal LA9 6NH
Tel: (01539) 726624

Margaret Malcolm, Development
Manager
**Fylde Industry Education
Federation (FIEF) Ltd**
Partnership Link
Croston House
Lancashire Enterprises Business
Park
Centurion Way
Leyland PR5 1TZ
Tel: (01772) 622030
Fax: (01772) 622656

Neil Mawdsley
Hyndburn, Ribble Valley &
   Rossendale EBP
GEC Clayton Business Park
Clayton le Moors BB5 5JW
Tel: (01254) 389898
Fax: (01254) 239084

Tony Gill, EBP Project Manager
Kendal and South Lakes EBP
37 Beast Banks
Kendal LA9 4JJ
Tel: (01539) 725072
Fax: (01539) 725072

Deborah McGoldrick,
   Development Manager
Lancashire and District Business
   Education Liaison (LADBEL)
   Ltd
Partnership Link
Croston House
Lancashire Enterprises Business
   Park
Centurion Way
Leyland PR5 1TZ
Tel: (01722) 622030
Fax: (01772) 622656

Mary Connery, Chief Executive
Manchester EBP Ltd
The Paul Building
Denison Road
Victoria Park
Manchester M14 5RX
Tel: (0161) 2560120
Fax: (0161) 2560118

Jayne Dickens, EBP Manager
North & Mid Cheshire TEC
Spencer House
Dewhurst Road
Warrington
Cheshire WA3 7PP
Tel: (01925) 826515
Fax: (01925) 820215
E-mail: general@normid.u-net.com

Diane Mellor, Education Manager
Oldham CCTE
Meridian Centre, King Street
Oldham OL8 1EZ
Tel: (0161) 620 0006
Fax: (0161) 620 0030

Clive Gee, COMPACT/EBP
   Manager
Oldham COMPACT/EBP
Centre for Professional
   Development
Rosary Road, Fitton Hill
Oldham OL8 2QE
Tel: (0161) 9114224
Fax: (0161) 9114250
E-mail: cg@oldhamcompact.
   demon.co.uk

Marie Finney, General Manager
Partnership Link (Lancashire Area
   West)
Partnership Link
Croston House
Lancashire Enterprises Business
   Park
Centurion Way
Leyland PR5 1TZ
Tel: (01772) 622030
Fax: (01772) 622656

Neil Mawdsley
Pendle EBP (serviced by East
   Lancs)
GEC Clayton Business Park
Clayton le Moors
Accrington BB5 5JW
Tel: (01254) 389898
Fax: (01254) 239084

Fiona Hilton, Education Manager
Rochdale Borough CCTE
St James Place
160–162 Yorkshire Street
Rochdale OL16 2DL
Tel: (0170) 664 4909
Fax: (0170) 664 9979
E-mail: t.nunn@rbccte.co.uk

Peter Collins, EBP Director
Salford EBP
Business and Technology Centre
Green Lane
Patricroft
Manchester M30 0RJ
Tel: (0161) 7873135
Fax: (0161) 7873137

Alison Turner, Education Strategy
    Manager
South and East Cheshire BEP
PO Box 37
Dalton Way
Middlewich
Cheshire CW10 0HU
Tel: (01606) 734218
Fax: (01606) 734201

Tony Gill, EBP Project Manager
South Lakes EBP
Lake District Business Park
Mint Bridge Road
Kendal LA9 6NH
Tel: (01539) 726624

Sue Eldridge/Harry Unsworth,
    EBP Manager
Stockport/High Peak EBP
c/o Stockport/High Peak TEC
1 St Peters Square
Stockport
Cheshire SK1 1NN
Tel: (0161) 4778830
Fax: (0161) 4804956
E-mail: suee@shptec.co.uk
E-mail: harry@.shptec.co.uk

Bill Twiss, EBP Manager
Tameside EBP
Acorn House
Albert Street
Droylsden
Manchester M43 7BA
Tel: (0161) 371 5777
Fax: (0161) 370 9409

Martin Lester, Executive Director
Trafford BEP
Lloyd House
392 Third Avenue
Trafford Park
Manchester M17 1JE
Tel: (0161) 8484305
Fax: (0161) 8484323

Linda Smye, EBP Project Manager
West Cumbria EBP
Venture House
Guard Street
Workington
Cumbria CA14 4EW
Tel: (01900) 66991
Fax: (01900) 604027

Clive Moss, EBP Manager
**Wigan Borough Partnership
    Training & Enterprise Ltd**
Wigan Investment Centre
Waterside Drive
Wigan WN3 5BA
Tel: (01942) 705705
Fax: (01942) 705490

Scotland

Andrea Tyrer, Co-ordinator
Dunbartonshire & Lomand EBP
4 South Crosshill Road
Bishopbriggs
Glasgow G64 2NN
Tel: (0141) 772 5099
Fax: (0141) 772 5684
E-mail: ebp@dlcsp.org.uk

Valerie Treneman, EBP Manager
Shetland Enterprise
Toll Clock Shopping Centre
Lerwick
Shetland ZE1 0DE
Tel: (01595) 693177
Fax: (01595) 693208

Sc HIE

Wilma Clark, Manager
Argyll & Bute EBP
Drummore Education
    Development Centre
Soroba Road, Oban
Argyll A34 4SN
Tel: (01631) 566726
Fax: (01631) 564615
E-mail: ebp.aie@hient.co.uk

Simon Moodie, Manager/Secretary
Caithness & Sutherland EBP
Scapa House, Castlegreen Road
Thurso
Caithness KW14 7LS
Tel: (01847) 896115
Fax: (01847) 893383

Iain MacKintosh, Manager
Inverness & Nairn, Badenoch &
    Strathspey EBP
Central Primary School
Kenneth Street
Inverness IV3 5DW
Tel: (01463) 225449
Fax: (01463) 663809
E-mail: iain_mackintosh@hcs.fc.
    uhi.ak.uk

Eric McKenzie, Manager
Lochaber EBP
Lochaber Opportunities Centre
An Aird
Fort William PH33 6AN
Tel: (01397) 701170
Fax: (01397) 701886

Bill Graham, Manager
Moray EBP
Moray Park, Findhorn Road
Forres
Moray IV36 0TP
Tel: (01309) 672793
Fax: (01309) 671272
E-mail: mebp@carvic.demon.co.uk
Web site: www.carvic.demon.co.uk
    /mebp

Alasdair MacLeod, Manager
Orkney EBP
Orkney Opportunities Centre
The Brig
2 Albert Street
Kirkwall
Orkney KW15 1HP
Tel: (01856) 872460
Fax: (01856) 875515

Moira Anderson, Manager
Ross & Cromarty EBP
62 High Street
Invergordon
Ross-shire IV18 0DH
Tel: (01349) 853666
Fax: (01349) 853833
E-mail: m.anderson@hient.co.uk

Valerie Treneman, Manager
Shetland EBP
Toll Clock Shopping Centre
20 North Road
Lerwick
Shetland ZE1 0DE
Tel: (01595) 693177
Fax: (01595) 693208

Helen Richardson, Co-ordinator
Skye & Lochalsh EBP
Craggan Cottage
Balmacara by Kyle of Lochalsh
IV40 8DN
Tel: (01599) 566231
Fax: (01599) 566231
Web site: www.ebp.org.uk

Iain Stewart, Manager
Western Isles EBP
Haldane Centre
Church Street
Stornoway
Isle of Lewis
Tel: (01851) 703564
Fax: (01851) 704709
E-mail: wislesebp@aol.com.
Web site: www.eulas.co.uk/

ScSEN

Patricia Young, EIL Projects
  Officer
Angus EBP
Angus Council Education
  Development Service
Bruce House
Wellgate
Arbroath DD11 3TE
Tel: (01241) 435022
Fax: (01241) 435034
E-mail: eilangus@sol.co.uk

John Curran, Manager
Ayrshire EBP
Education Business Centre
Building 94
British Aerospace and
  Aerostructure
Prestwick International Airport
Prestwick KT9 2RW
Tel: (01563) 545150
Fax: (01563) 572577
E-mail: john.curran@scot.ent.co.uk

Terry West, Manager
Dumfries and Galloway EBP
Lochside Education Centre
Lochside Road
Dumfries DG2 0EL
Tel: (01387) 720774
Fax: (01387) 721276
E-mail: dumfriesandgall@campus.
  bt.com

Robbie Mackintosh, Head of
  Human Resource Development
**Dumfries and Galloway Enterprise
  Co Ltd**
Tinwald Downs Road
Dumfries Enterprise Park
Heathall
Dumfries DG1 3SJ
Tel: (01387) 245000
Fax: (01387) 246224

Mhairi Robertson, Life Long
  Learning Project Leader
Dunbartonshire EBP
Spectrum House
North Avenue
Clydebank Business Park
Glasgow G81 2DR
Tel: (0141) 951 2121
Fax: (0141) 951 1907
E-mail: mhairirobertson@
  scotent.co.uk

Graham Stevenson
**Dundee Education Industry
  Partnership Education
  Development Service**
Gardyne Road
Dundee DD1 1NY
Tel: (01382) 462857
Fax: (01382) 462862

Hazel Mathieson, Manager
Fife Enterprise
Fast Trac
Kingdom House
Saltire Centre
Glenrothes KY6 2AQ
Tel: (01592) 623152
Fax: (01592) 623199
E-mail: hazel.mathieson@scotent.
  co.uk

Patricia Thompson, Manager
Forth Valley EBP
Rooms 45 & 46
Haypark Business Centre
Marchmont Avenue
Polmont FK2 0NZ
Tel: (01324) 718414
Fax: (01324) 715686
E-mail: fvebp@post.almac.co.uk
Web site: www.heartofscotland.
  co.uk

Alex Blackwood, Manager
Glasgow EBP Partnership Centre
67 Abbey Drive
Jordanhill G14 9JW
Tel: (0141) 954 1999
Fax: (0141) 950 2117
E-mail: Glasgow-ebp@cqm.co.uk

Isobel Maughan, Manager
Grampian EBP
27 Albyn Place
Aberdeen AB1 1DG
Tel: (01224) 575100
Fax: (01224) 213417
E-mail: fiona.preston@scotent.co.uk

Stuart Macfarlane, Manager
Lanarkshire EBP Resource Centre
Caldervale High School
Airdrie ML6 8PJ
Tel: (01236) 762485
Fax: (01236) 767250
E-mail: stuartmacfarlane@scot.
ent.co.uk

Alasdair Ferguson, Manager
**Lothian EBP Career Development
Edinburgh and Lothians**
Atholl House
2 Canning Street
Edinburgh EH3 8EG
Tel: (0131) 228 7537
Fax: (0131) 228 3146
E-mail: alasdair@lothianebp.
demon.co.uk

Maureen Campbell, Manager
Perth and Kinross EBP
Highland House
St Catherines Road
Perth PH1 5RY
Tel: (01738) 629457
Fax: (01738) 445138

John Sweeney, EBP Manager
Renfrewshire EBP
27 Causeyside Street
Paisley PA1 1UL
Tel: (0141) 842 3584
Fax: (0141) 848 6930
E-mail: john.sweeney@rebp.co.uk

South East

Anna Jury, EBP Manager
Ashford EBP
c/o Quest International UK Ltd
Ashford
Kent TN24 0LT
Tel: (01233) 644782
Fax: (01233) 644484

Penny Askew/Geoff Stubbs, EBP
Managers
Aylesbury Vale EBP
County Hall
Aylesbury
Buckinghamshire HP20 1UZ
Tel: (01296) 382708
Fax: (01296) 382383
E-mail: avebp@buckscc.gov.uk

Terry Martin
Canterbury EBP
c/o 15 Old Bridge Road
Whitstable
Kent CT5 1RJ
Tel: (01227) 770648/277693
Fax: (01227) 277898

Geoff Stubbs, EBP Manager
Chiltern & S Bucks EBP
Education Office
King Geroge V Road
Amersham
Buckinghamshire HP6 5BY
Tel: (01494) 732119
Fax: (01494) 732922
E-mail: csbebp@buckscc.gov.uk

Mike Mason, EBP Manager
COUNTEC Ltd
Tempus
249 Midsummer Boulevard
Milton Keynes MK9 1EU
Tel: (01908) 660005
Fax: (01908) 230130
E-mail: masonm@mk-chamber.
co.uk

Matthew Hedges, EBP Manager
Dartford/Swanley EBP
c/o Dartford Borough Council
Civic Centre
Dartford
Kent DA1 1DR
Tel: (01322) 343000
Fax: (01322) 343422

John Holmes
Dover/Deal EBP
c/o White Cliffs Business Park
Honeywood Road
Whitfield
Dover
Kent CT13 3EH
Tel: (01304) 827027
Fax: (01304) 822354

Gerry Shaw
East Oxfordshire EBP
Woodeaton Manor School
Woodeaton OX3 9TS
Tel: (01865) 316170

Tim Sorensen
East Sussex EBP (covering East
Sussex, Brighton and Hove)
Curriculum Development Division
Sussex Careers Services HQ
The Rise
Portslade BN41 2PY
Tel: (01273) 704106
Fax: (01273) 708912
E-mail: 101356.463@compuserve.
com

Angela Wright, Manager
**Eastleigh Action for Skills
  Enterprise and Learning Ltd**
Wessex House
Upper Market Street
Eastleigh
Hampshire SO50 9FD
Tel: (023) 8065 2118
Fax: (023) 8065 2122

Roger Buck, Manager
First Partnership Limited
Education Business Partnership
  Centre
Mayhill Junior School
The Bury
Odiham
Hampshire RG29 1NB
Tel: (01256) 701294
Fax: (01256) 703955
E-mail: first_partnership@yahoo.
com

John Cherry, Manager
Gravesham BEP
c/o Britannia Refined Metals
  Limited
Botany Road
Northfleet
Gravesend
Kent DA11 9BG
Tel: (01474) 353608
Fax: (01474) 353609

Shelagh Rolland, Manager
Hastings and Rye EBP
Summerfields Business Centre
Bohemia Road
Hastings
East Sussex TN34 1UT
Tel: (01424) 781757/9
Fax: (01424) 781757
E-mail: shelagh.rolland
    @sussexenterprise.co.uk

Margaret Pearson, General
   Manager
Kent EBP
26 Kings Hill Avenue
Kings Hill
West Malling
Kent ME19 4AE
Tel: (01732) 220111
Fax: (01732) 220222
E-mail: kebp@kent.businesslink.
   co.uk
Web site: www.setpointse.com

Jenny Asher, EBP Manager
Maidenhead EBP
Altwood School
Altwood Road
Maidenhead SL6 4PU
Tel: (01628) 637348
Fax: (01628) 788331

Alan Mount
Mid Kent EBP
Mid Kent College
Oakwood Park
Tonbridge Road
Maidstone
Kent ME16 8AQ
Tel: (01622) 763004
Fax: (01622) 695049

Alan Vincent
**North Oxfordshire Learning
   Partnership**
9 Lawrence Leys
Bloxham
Banbury OX15 4NU
Tel: (01295) 720809
Fax: (01295) 720809

Terry Hammersley
Oxford City EBP
Cricket Road Centre
Cricket Road
Oxford OX4 3DW
Tel: (01865) 747038
Fax: (01865) 747675

Pat Finlay, EBP Manager
Oxfordshire EBP
Partnership Unit
Cricket Road Centre, Cricket Road
Oxford OX4 3DW
Tel: (01865) 428051
Fax: (01865) 428050

Marie Gaylard, Partnership
   Manager
**Portsmouth & South East Hants
   EBP Ltd**
4th Floor
Regional Business Centre
Baltic House
Kingston Crescent
Portsmouth
Hampshire PO2 8QL
Tel: (023) 9267 7444
Fax: (023) 9266 7115

Anne Wilson, EBP Manager
Reading EBP
PO Box 2134
Civic Centre
Reading RG1 7DG
Tel: (01189) 504434
Fax: (01189) 509894

Judith Skinner
Shepway EBP
c/o SIMS Portex Ltd
1–3 High Street
Hythe
Kent CT21 5AB
Tel: (01303) 260551
Fax: (01303) 262248

Geoffrey Bateman, Operations
   Manager
**Skills Training and Enterprise
   Partnership Limited**
Wessex Chambers, South Street
Andover
Hampshire SP10 2BN
Tel: (01264) 333868
Fax: (01264) 338055
E-mail: skills@worldhq.com

Evelyn Hill, EBP Manager
South East Berkshire EBP
Bracknell Forest Council
Edward Elgar House
Skimped Hill Lane
Bracknell RG12 1LY
Tel: (01344) 354074
Fax: (01344) 354004

Andrea McPhail, Manager
South East Oxfordshire EBP
Henley College
Deanfield Avenue
Henley on Thames RG9 1UH
Tel: (01491) 579988 Ext 338
Fax: (01189) 263836

Christine Pickavance, Manager
South Oxfordshire EBP
82 Milton Park
Abingdon
Oxon OX14 4RY
Tel: (01235) 832559

The Manager
**Southampton & Forest Headstart
    Limited**
Wheatsheaf House
24 Bernard Street
Southampton
Hampshire SO14 3AY
Tel: (023) 8023 7662
Fax: (023) 8023 7651

Roy Gouriet, Manager
Surrey EBP
2a Merrow Business Centre
Merrow Lane
Guildford GU4 7WA
Tel: (01483) 457111
Fax: (01483) 531866

Karen Harbour, Manager
Sussex Enterprise
Greenacre Court, Station Road
Burgess Hill RH15 9DS
Tel: (01444) 259111
Fax: (01444) 259127

James Brown, Manager
Swale TEBP
Swale Business Centre
East Street
Sittingbourne
Kent ME10 3HT
Tel: (01795) 417226
Fax: (01795) 417240
E-mail: info@swale-chamber.org.uk

Anne McNulty, EBP Manager
Thanet EBP
Thanet Business Centre
Victoria Road
Margate
Kent CT9 1LW
Tel: (01843) 233416
Fax: (01843) 293822

Julie Standen, Manager
**The Basingstoke Consortium
    Limited**
John Hunt of Everest School
Popley Way
Basingstoke
Hampshire RG24 9AB
Tel: (01256) 840710
Fax: (01256) 811634

Lyn Hargood, EBP Manager
West Berkshire EBP
Newbury College
Oxford Road
Newbury
Berkshire RG14 1PQ
Tel: (01635) 32931
Fax: (01635) 528198
E-mail: wbebp@clara.net

Cathy Gaunt, EBP Manager
West Kent EBP
West Kent Business Centre
River Walk
Tonbridge
Kent TN9 1DT
Tel: (07957) 208506
Fax: (07957) 208506

Sue Samson, EBP Manager
West Sussex EBP
Education Department
County Hall
Chichester PO19 1RF
Tel: (01243) 777267
Fax: (01243) 777791

Malcolm Lloyd, Operations
    Manager
Wight TEC
Mill Court
Furlongs
Newport
Isle of Wight PO30 2AA
Tel: (01983) 822818

Sandra Wooledge, EBP Manager
Windsor Slough EBP
c/o SmithKline Beecham
11 Stoke Poges Lane
Slough
Berkshire SL1 3NW
Tel: (01753) 502384
Fax: (01753) 502385

Penny Askew, EBP Manager
Wycombe Education Business Unit
Wycombe Area Office
Easton Street
High Wycombe HP11 1NH
Tel: (01494) 475343
Fax: (01494) 475001
E-mail: wycebu@buckscc.gov.uk

South West

Rick Hatton, EBP Manager
Bath & North East Somerset EBP
14 Queens Square
Bath BA1 2HN
Tel: (01225) 461501
Fax: (01225) 465619

Lois Thorn, EBP Manager
Bristol EBP
Learning Partnership West
4 Colston Avenue
Bristol BS1 4ST
Tel: (0117) 9873700
Fax: (0117) 9074519

Jill King, Work Related Activities
    Manager
Central EBP
Learning Partnership West
4 Colston Avenue
Bristol BS1 4ST
Tel: (01179) 9872444
Fax: (01179) 9874518

Heather Lee, EBP Manager
Cheltenham & Cotswolds EBP
c/o Eagle Star Centre
Montpellier Drive
Cheltenham GL53 7LQ
Tel: (01242) 221335
Fax: (01242) 221554

David Smith, EBP Manager
Cornwall EBP
Dalvenie House
New County Hall
Truro
Cornwall TR1 3BA
Tel: (01872) 323420
Fax: (01872) 323806

J Ann Forsyth, EBP Director
Devon EBP
First Floor
ABC House
Venny Bridge
Pinhoe
Exeter EX4 8JH
Tel: (01392) 462288
Fax: (01392) 462266
E-mail: partnership@devonebp.
    demon.co.uk

Tony Boyden, EBP Manager
Dorset EBP
Winfrith Technology Centre
Dorchester
Dorset DT2 8DH
Tel: (01305) 853992
Fax: (01305) 853995
E-mail: dorsetebp@enterprise.net

Ros Daniels, EBP Manager
Forest EBP
6/6F The Mews, Brook Street
Mitcheldean
Gloucester GL17 0SL
Tel: (01594) 544951
Fax: (01594) 544510
E-mail: ros@ebp-forest-
glos.demon.co

Janet Hembry, EBP Manager
Gloucester EBP
Conway House
33–35 Worcester Street
Gloucester
Gloucestershire GL1 3AJ
Tel: (01452) 524488
Fax: (01452) 509678

Paul Delbridge-Smith, EBP
Manager
Isles of Scilly EBP
Isles of Scilly School
St Mary's
Isles of Scilly TR21 0RY
Tel: (01720) 422929
Fax: (01720) 422929

Dr Ian Whittle
Mid Gloucestershire EBP
6 Torchacre Close
Dursley
Gloucestershire GL11 4LW
Tel: (01453) 543173

Steve Hodges, EBP Manager
North Somerset EBP
45 Boulevard
Weston-super-Mare BS23 9PG
Tel: (01934) 644443
Fax: (01934) 6444409

John Crew, EBP Manager
**Somerset Education Business
Centre**
Crescent House
The Mount
Taunton
Somerset TA1 3TT
Tel: (01823) 320330
Fax: (01823) 336246

Maggie Moss, EBP Manager
South Gloucestershire EBP
28–30 Gloucester Road
Filton
Bristol BS7 0SJ
Tel: (0117) 9695808
Fax: (0117) 9312978

Carol Endacott
Stroud EBP
c/o Maidenhill School
Kings Road
Stonehouse
Stroud GL10 2HA
Tel: (01453) 825639

Richard Cummins, Business
Liaison Manager
Swindon EBP
Sanford House
Sanford Street
Swindon SN1 1QH
Tel: (01793) 463052
Fax: (01793) 488597

Helen Hopkins
EBP Manager
Tamar EBP
Seymour House
Mount Wise
Plymouth PL1 4JQ
Tel: (01752) 605608
Fax: (01752) 605635
E-mail: tebp@tebp.devon-cc.gov.
uk

Joan Lardy, Projects Manager
Wiltshire & Swindon TEC
The Bora Building
Westlea Campus
Westlea Down
Swindon
Wiltshire SN5 7EZ
Tel: (01793) 513644
Fax: (01793) 542006

West

Hywel Wyn Jones
EBP Manager
St Asaph Business Park
St Asaph
Denbighshire
Tel: (01745) 538500
E-mail: hywel.wyn.jones@celtec.
co.uk

Ina Standish, EBP Coordinator
Blaenau Gwent EBP
Victoria House
Victoria Business Park
Festival Park
Ebbw Vale NP3 6ER
Tel: (01495) 311008
Fax: (01495) 312307

Ros Adams
Executive Committee Business
Centre
William Knox House
Britannia Way
Llandarcy
Neath SA10 6EL
Tel: (01792) 352000
Fax: (01792) 817770

June Davies, EBP Coordinator
Caerphilly EBP
Woodfieldside Business Centre
Woodfieldside Business Park
Penmaen Road
Pontllanfraith NP2 2DG
Tel: (01495) 235608
Fax: (01495) 232712

Rita Deegan, EBP Manager
Career Paths
53 Charles Street
Cardiff CF1 4ED
Tel: (029) 2025 5780
Fax: (029) 2025 5798

Philip Drakeford, EBP Manager
Dyfed EBP
13 Anthony Way
Cillefwr Industrial Estate
Johnstown
Carmarthen
Dyfed SA31 3RB
Tel: (01267) 231387
Fax: (01267) 226949
E-mail: p.drakeford@dyfedebp.
org.uk

Jane Smith, EBP Manager
Gwent TEC
Education Business Section
Cleppa Park
Newport
Gwent NP1 9BA
Tel: (01633) 817777
Fax: (01633) 810980

Keith Gillard, EBP Chief
Executive
Mid Glamorgan EBP
Taff Ely Teachers' Centre
The Broadway
Pontypridd
Mid Glamorgan CF37 1BE
Tel: (01443) 409174
Fax: (01443) 406566

Frances Harding, EBP
Coordinator
Monmouth EBP
County Hall
Cwmbran NP44 2XH
Tel: (01633) 644516
Fax: (01633) 644488

Pam Harper, EBP Coordinator
Newport EBP
Bettws High School
Bettws Lane
Newport NP9 5XL
Tel: (01633) 854351
Fax: (01633) 821495

Audrey Guy, Director of
    Education
Powys TEC
1st Floor, St David's House
Newtown
Powys SY19 1RB
Tel: (0168) 662 2494
Fax: (0168) 662 2716
E-mail: frankg@powys.tec.org.uk

Mike Money
South Glamorgan Career Paths
53 Charles Street
Cardiff CF1
Tel: (01222) 255780
Fax: (01222) 255798

Education Manager
South Glamorgan TEC
2–7 Drake Walk
Brigantine Place
Atlantic Wharf
Cardiff CF1 5AN
Tel: (029) 2022 61000
Fax: (029) 2024 50424

Christine Chapman/Ian Freebury,
    EBP Coordinator
Torfaen EBP
Third Floor
County Hall
Cwmbran
Tel: (01633) 648156
Fax: (01633) 648159

West Midlands

Gill Adderley, Manager
Birmingham East Partnership
East Birmingham College
Garretts Green Lane
Birmingham B33 0TS
Tel: (0121) 742 2410
Fax: (0121) 742 2410

Mary Davies, Chief Executive
**Careers and Education Business
    Partnership**
Charter House
100 Broad Street
Birmingham B15 1AE
Tel: (0121) 248 8000
Fax: (0121) 248 8001
Web site: www.cebp.co.uk

Adrian Booth, EBP Manager
Coventry EBP
c/o Elmbank Teachers' Centre
Mile Lane
Coventry CV1 2LQ
Tel: (024) 7652 7478
Fax: (024) 7652 7469

Dudley Light, Education Manager
Dudley TEC
3 Dudley Court South
Waterfront Street
Level Street
Brierley Hill
Dudley DY5 1XN
Tel: (01384) 485000
Fax: (01384) 483399

Eileen Stead, EBP Area Manager
EBP Worcestershire
MCF Complex
New Road
Kidderminster
Worcestershire
West Midlands DY10 1AQ
Tel: (01562) 828 2000
Fax: (01562) 877 555

Geoff Heaps, Manager
Erdington Partnership
Josiah Mason College
Slade Road
Erdington
Birmingham B23 7JH
Tel: (0121) 382 2813/2918
Fax: (0121) 382 1357

Anton Jacobus, EBP Manager
Hereford EBP
Carfax House
Folly Lane
Hereford HR1 1HR
Tel: (01432) 342865
Fax: (01432) 342865

Barrie Cannings, Partnership
Manager
Impact Partnership
Bournville College of FE
Bristol Road South
Northfield
Birmingham B31 2AJ
Tel: (0121) 476 5918
Fax: (0121) 476 5918

Shannon Moore, Manager
Laser Partnership
The Care & Early Years Education
& Training Centre
Pitmaston Road
Hall Green
Birmingham B28 9PW
Tel: (0121) 694 5405
Fax: (0121) 694 5406
E-mail: laser@sbirmc.co.uk

Gay Jones, Manager
Norlink/Sutton Partnerships
North Birmingham College
Aldridge Road
Great Barr
Birmingham B44 8NE
Tel: (0121) 366 6733
Fax: (0121) 366 6507

Mary B. McGrath, EBP Manager
Sandwell EBP
1st Floor Black Country House
Rounds Green Road
Oldbury
West Bromwich
West Midlands B69 2DG
Tel: (0121) 5432222
Fax: (0121) 5434444

Richard Jeary, Business Education
Manager
**Shropshire Chamber of Comm.
Training and Enterprise**
Trevithick House
Stafford Park 4
Telford
Shropshire TF3 3BA
Tel: (01952) 208200
Fax: (01952) 208208
E-mail: rjeary@shropshire-
chamber.co.uk

Barbara Birks, Contact
Solihull EBP
Central Careers
6 The Square
Warwick Court
Solihull B91 3RB
Tel: (0121) 605 3444
Fax: (0121) 605 3434

Anne Preston, Director
Staffordshire Partnership/TEC
PO Box 33
Lichfield Road
Stafford
Staffordshire ST17 4LN
Tel: (01785) 274878/859
Fax: (01785) 256680
E-mail: staffpart@staffordshire.
gov.uk

Peter Crewe, Manager
Titan Partnership
St George's Post 16 Centre
Great Hampton Row
Newtown
Birmingham B19 3JG
Tel: (0121) 212 4567
Fax: (0121) 233 3388

John Price, EBP Manager
Walsall EBP
5th Floor, Townend House
Townend Square
Walsall
West Midlands WS1 1NS
Tel: (01922) 424200
Fax: (01922) 424243

John Botten, EBP Manager
Warwickshire EBP
Manor Hall, Sandy Lane
Leamington Spa
Warwickshire CV32 6RD
Tel: (01926) 413777
Fax: (01926) 413773
E-mail: johnbotten@
    warwickshire.gov.uk

Julie James, Education Manager
Wolverhampton CCTE
Pendeford Business Park
Wobaston Road
Wolverhampton WV9 5HA
Tel: (0190) 244 5500
Fax: (0190) 244 5200

Yorkshire & Humberside

Linda Burgess, EBP Manager
Barnsley BEP
Education Business Centre
Dodworth Junior School
Barnsley Road
Dodworth
Barnsley S75 3JS
Tel: (01226) 285917
Fax: (01226) 287644
E-mail: barnsleybep@btinternet.com

Michael Lowe, Education Manager
Bradford & District TEC
Mercury House
4 Manchester Road
Bradford
West Yorkshire BD5 0QL
Tel: (0127) 475 1333
Fax: (0127) 475 1344

Andrew Czolacz, Chief Executive
**Compact Education Business
    Services**
c/o Batley High School for Boys
Field Hill
Batley WF17 0BJ
Tel: (01924) 326328
Fax: (01924) 423250
E-mail: compact-ebs@geo2.
    poptel.org.uk

Alan Hendry, EBP Co-ordinator
Doncaster EBP
Professional Development Centre
Carr House Centre, Danum Road
Doncaster DN4 5HF
Tel: (01302) 734714
Fax: (01302) 734713

Dr Wendy Richardson, Business
    Education Director
Humberside Partnership
(Business Education Links
    Directorate)
Foster House
Stoneferry Park
Foster Street
Hull HU8 8BT
Tel: (01482) 588645
Fax: (01482) 588714

Norah Keany, EBP Manager
Leeds TEC
Belgrave Hall
Belgrave Street
Leeds LS2 8DD
Tel: (0113) 2285275
Fax: (0113) 2438126
E-mail: nk@leedstec.co.uk

Diane Christon, BEP Manager
North Yorkshire BEP (NYBEP)
Spitfire House
Aviator Court
York YO30 4UZ
Tel: (01904) 693632
Fax: (01904) 693070
E-mail: partnership@nybep.
    demon.co.uk
Web site: www.nybep.demon.
    co.uk

Steven Hanstock
Business Education Links
Rotherham Chamber of
    Commerce, Training and
    Education
The Millside Centre
Doncaster Road
Dalton
Rotherham S65 3ET
Tel: (01709) 855550 Ext 18
Fax: (01709) 855551

Deirdre Eastburn, EBP Manager
Sheffield EBP
Education Department
Leopold Street
Sheffield S1 1RJ
Tel: (0114) 2727544
Fax: (0114) 2786641
E-mail: dae@sebp.demon.co.uk
Web site: www.sebp.demon.
    co.uk

Catherine Lunn, Education/EBP
    Manager
Wakefield TEC
Grove Hall
60 College Grove Road
Wakefield
West Yorkshire WF1 3RN
Tel: (01924) 299907
Fax: (01924) 201837
E-mail: catherine.lunn@
    wakefield-tec.co.uk

Appendix 2:
The Internet

30 free-to-join affiliate reseller programmes

Wealth creation
The Duplicator *http://www.theduplicator.com/vip/cgi/jim333*
Active Marketplace *http://activemarketplace.com/w.cgi?winning-6556*
Six Figure Income *http://www.sixfigureincome.com/?122341*
IPRO *http://iprolinks.com/affiliates/jim333*
Private profits *http://www.privateprofits.com*

Communications
Virtualis *http://www.virtualis.com/vr2/jgreen2*
VenerNet *http://www.vener.net/rep2/jimgreen-info.shtm*
RealCall *http://www.realcall.net/internet*
Cognigen *http://LD.net/?sing333*
Global Planet *http://LD.net/bizop/?jim333*
My Free Office *http://www.myfreeoffice.com/jimswebstore.html*
Hotyellow98 *http://hotyellow98.com/jimgreen/jimswebstore.html*
EzzeNet *http://www.ezze.net/affiliates/28699*

Internet training
Site Sell *http://www.sitesell.com/success66.html*

Electronic publishing
Insider Internet Marketing *http://www.bizweb2000.com/d5315.htm*

Software
Marketsize *http://www.marketwize.com/biz/ware/m45r/index.html*
Multilinks *http://multilinks.net/index.shtml?10966*
Smart Money Group *http://www.smartmoneygroup.com/SMG/ ghostmem?JGO152.htm*
Postmaster *http://www.post-master.net/rs/jimswebstore*
Aweber *http://www.aweber.com/?14553*

Educational
Internet Marketing Challenge *http://www.marketingchallenge.com/index.cgi?15053*
Magic Learning *http://www.magiclearning.com/cgi/members/JG51079*

Online shopping
Kosoma *http://www.kosoma.com/welcome/d1045cash/BestAd.html*
Gold Club *http://www.gold-club.net/cgi-bin/sponsor.asp?JG26154*
Spree *http://www.spree.com*

Personals
One and Only Network *http://www.one-and-only.com/menu1.htm?MID = 203360*

Credit Cards
Next Card *http://cognigen.net/getnext.cgi*

Banking
Clickbank *http://www.clickbank.com/jim333*

Gaming
Silver Dollar Casino *http://www.gamblingfever.net/members/SilverDollar/index.shtml*

Books
Amazon *http://www.amazon.co.uk*

20 free e-mail facilities
Conk?Mail *http://conk.com*
Hotmail *http://hotmail.com*
TheMail *http://www.themail.com*
LYCOS *http://lycosemail.com*
MailCity *http://mailcity.com*
MailExcite *http://mailexcite.com*
MrPost *http://mrpost.com*
Net@ddress *http://netaddress.usa.net*
Yahoo Mail *http://mail.yahoo.com*
Eudora Web-Mail *http://eudoramail.com*
FlasheMail *http://flashemail.com*
Postmaster *http://postmaster.co.uk*
ProntoMail *http://onlymail.com*
SoftHome *http://softhome.com*
SUPERNEWS *http://supernews.com*
Hempseed *http://hempseed.com*
My Own Email *http://myownemail.com*
GoPlay *http://goplay.com*
Juno *http://juno.com*

Business Address Book

A short book of this kind can only be a guide to the way to set up a business of your own. You will no doubt need further information and advice on starting your business, running it, and expanding in the future. To help you find that information and advice, here is a comprehensive list of contacts which may be of help.

STARTING UP

Business in the Community, 8 Stratton Street, London W1X 6AH. Tel: (020) 7629 1600.

Companies Registration Office, 55 City Road, London EC1Y 1BB. Tel: (020) 7253 9393. Also at: Companies House, Crown Way, Cardiff CF4 3UZ. Tel: (01222) 388588.

Council for Small Industries in Rural Areas, 141 Castle Street, Salisbury, Wiltshire SP1 3TP. Tel: (01722) 336255.

Department of Trade and Industry (DTI), 1-19 Victoria Street, London SW1Y 0ET. Tel: (020) 7215 7877.

DTI Loan Guarantee Section, Level 2, St Mary's House, c/o Moorfoot, Sheffield S1 4PQ. Tel: (0114) 2597308/9.

National Business Names Registry, Somerset House, Temple Street, Birmingham B5 2DP. Tel: (0121) 643 0227.

Prince's Youth Business Trust, 5 Cleveland Place, London SW1Y 6JJ. Tel: (020) 7925 2900.

Small Firms Information Service, Abell House, John Islip Street, London SW1P 4LN. Dial 100 and ask for FREEPHONE ENTERPRISE.

Registrar of Business Names, London Chamber of Commerce, 33 Queen Street, London EC4R 1BX. Tel: (020) 7248 4444.

Registrar of Companies, 21 Bothwell Street, Glasgow G2 6NL. Tel: (0141) 248 3315.

Wyvern Business Library, 6 The Business Park, Ely, Cambridgeshire CB7 4JW. Tel: (01352) 665544. Supplies a range of practical business and self improvement books by direct mail.

MEMBERSHIP ORGANISATIONS

Alliance of Small Firms and Self-Employed People Ltd, 33 The Greene, Calne, Wiltshire SN11 8DJ. Tel: (01249) 817003.

The Association of British Chambers of Commerce, 9 Tufton Street, London SW1P 3QB. Tel: (020) 7222 1555.

Business Link. Tel: 0800 104010. Business support services.

Federation of Small Businesses, 32 Orchard Road, Lytham St Annes FY8 1NY. Tel: (01253) 720911.

Association of Independent Businesses, 26 Addison Place, London W11 4RJ. Tel: (020) 7371 1299.

British Franchise Association, Thames View, Newton Road, Henley on Thames, Oxfordshire RG9 1HG. Tel: (01491) 578049.

Confederation of British Industry, Centre Point, 103 Oxford Street, London WC1A 1DU. Tel: (020) 7379 7400.

Federation of Small Businesses, 140 Lower Marsh, Westminster Bridge, London SE1 7AE. Tel: (020) 7928 9272.

Institute of Directors, 116 Pall Mall, London SW1Y 5EA. Tel: (020) 7839 1233.

National Federation of Self Employed and Small Businesses, 32 St Annes Road West, Lytham St Annes, Lancashire FY8 1NY. Tel: (01253) 720911. And at:

Unit 101c Argent Centre, 60 Frederick Street, Birmingham B1 3HB. Tel: (0121) 236 6849.

11 Great George Street, Bristol, Avon BS1 5QY. Tel: (0117) 9276073.

34 Argyle Street, Glasgow G2 8BD. Tel: (0141) 221 0775.

35a Appletongate, Newark, Nottinghamshire NG24 1JR. Tel: (01636) 7101311.

National Market Traders' Federation, Hampton House, Hawshaw Lane, Hoyland, Barnsley, S74 0HA. Tel: (01226) 749021.

OwnBase, 68 First Avenue, Bush Hill Park, Enfield EN1 1BN. An organisation established to help people working from home.

RAISING FINANCE

Abbey National plc, Abbey House, Baker Street, London NW1 6XL. Tel: (020) 7486 5555.

American Express, PO Box 63, Brighton, Sussex BN1 1YZ. Tel: (01273) 696933.

Bank of Scotland, The Mound, Edinburgh EH1 1YZ. Tel: (0131) 243 5441.

Banking Information Service, 10 Lombard Street, London EC3V 9AT. Tel: (020) 7626 8486.

Barclays Banks PLC, 54 Lombard Street, London EC3N 3HJ. Tel: (020) 7626 1567.

Chartered Association of Certified Accountants, 29 Lincoln's Inn Fields, London WC2. Tel: (020) 7242 6855.

Clydesdale Bank PLC, 150 Buchanan Street, Glasgow G1. Tel: (0141) 248 7070.

Co-operative Bank PLC, PO Box 101, 1 Balloon Street, Manchester M60 4EP. Tel: (0161) 832 3456.

Finance and Leasing Association, 18 Upper Grosvenor Street, London W1X 9PB. Tel: (020) 7491 2783.

Institute of Chartered Accountants in England and Wales, PO Box 433, Chartered Accountants Hall, Moorgate Place, London EC2P 2BJ. Tel: (020) 7920 8100.

Institute of Chartered Accountants of Scotland, 27 Queen Street, Edinburgh EH2 1LA. Tel: (0131) 225 5673.

Institute of Management Consultants, 32 Hatton Garden, London EC1N 8DL. Tel: (020) 7242 2140.

Lloyds Bank PLC, PO Box 215, 71 Lombard Street, London EC3P 3BS. Tel: (020) 7626 1500.

Midland Bank PLC, 27 Poultry, London EC2P 2BX. Tel: (020) 7260 8000. Now a subsidiary of the Hong Kong & Shanghai Bank.

National Westminster Bank PLC, 41 Lothbury, London EC2P 2BP. Tel: (020) 7726 1000. It also owns Coutts & Co.

Nationwide Anglia Building Society, Chesterfield Road, Bloomsbury Way, London WC1V 6PW. Tel: (020) 7242 8822.

Office of the Banking Ombudsman, Citadel House, 5/11 Fetter Lane, London EC4A 1BR. Tel: (020) 7404 9944.

Royal Bank of Scotland, PO Box 31, 42 St Andrew Square, Edinburgh EH2 2YE. Tel: (0131) 556 8555.

3i PLC, 91 Waterloo Road, London SE1 8XP. Tel: (020) 7928 3131.

TSB Group PLC, 25 Milk Street, London EC2V 8LU. Tel: (020) 7606 7070.

MARKETING

Advertising Standards Authority, Brook House, Torrington Place, London WC1. Tel: (020) 7580 5555.

Advertising Association, Abford House, 15 Wilton Road, London SW1V 1NJ. Tel: (020) 7828 2771.

Association of Illustrators, 29 Bedford Square, London W1B 3EG. Tel: (020) 7636 4100.

British Media Publications, Windsor Court, East Grinstead House, East Grinstead, West Sussex RH19 1XE. Tel: (01342) 326972.

British Promotional Merchandise Association, 21-25 Lower Stone Street, Maidstone, Kent ME15 6YT. Tel: (01622) 671081.

Chartered Institute of Marketing, Moor Hall, Cookham, Berkshire SL6 9QH. Tel: (016285) 24922.

Communications, Advertising and Marketing Education Foundation, 15 Wilton Road, London SW1V 1NJ. Tel: (020) 7828 7506. For information about training.

Direct Mail Services Standards Board, 26 Eccleston Street, London SW1W 9PY. Tel: (020) 7824 8651.

Direct Marketing Association, Haymarket House, 1 Oxendon St, London SW1Y 4EE. Tel: (020) 7321 2525.

Direct Selling Association, 29 Floral Street, London WC2E 9DP. Tel: (020) 7497 1234.

Dun and Bradstreet, Holmers Farm Way, High Wycombe HP12 4UL. Tel: (01494) 422000. A leading provider of marketing and business information about individual companies.

Institute of Practitioners in Advertising, 44 Belgrave Square, London SW1X 8QS. Tel: (020) 7235 7020.

Institute of Public Relations, 15 Northburgh Street, London EC1V 0PR. Tel: (020) 7253 5151.

Institute of Sales Promotion, 66 Pentonville Road, London N1 9HS. Tel: (020) 7837 5340.

Market Research Society, 15 Northburgh Street, London EC1V 0AH. Tel: (020) 7490 4911.

Network Marketing Association, 5 Cornwall Crescent, London W11 1PH. Tel: (020) 221 5611.

Public Relations Consultants Association, Willow House, Willow Place, London SW1P 1JH. Tel: (020) 7233 6026.

LEGAL MATTERS

British Standards Institution, 2 Park Street, London W1A 2BS. Tel: (020) 7629 9000.

Data Protection Registrar, Springfield House, Water Lane, Wilmslow, Cheshire SK9 5AX. Tel: (01625) 535777.

Health and Safety Executive, St Hugh's House, Trinity Road, Bootle, Merseyside L20 2QY. Tel: (0151) 951 4381.

Rose Court, 2 Southwark Bridge, London SE1 9HS. Tel: (020) 7717 6000.

Broad Lane, Sheffield, Yorkshire S3 7HQ. Tel: (0114) 2892345.

Law Society (England and Wales), 113 Chancery Lane, London WC2A 1PL. Tel: (020) 7242 1222. The professional body for solicitors.

Law Society of Northern Ireland, 90-106 Victoria Street, Belfast BT1 2BJ. Tel: (028) 9023 1614.

Law Society of Scotland, 25 Drumsheugh Gardens, Edinburgh EH3 7YR. Tel: (0131) 226 7411.

Lawyers for Enterprise. Tel: (020) 7405 9075. These are solicitors who will offer a short, free initial interview concerning the general points you should consider when setting up or running a business.

Legal Aid Board, 8 Great New Street, London EC4A 3BN. Tel: (020) 7353 3794.

Office of Fair Trading, Field House, Breams Buildings, London EC4A 1HA. Tel: (020) 7242 2858.

Patent Office, 25 Southampton Buildings, Chancery Lane, London WC2A 1AY. Tel: (020) 7438 4700.

Royal Town Planning Institute, 26 Portland Place, London W1N 4BE. Tel: (020) 7636 9107.

The Trademarks Registry, 25 Southampton Buildings, Chancery Lane, London WC2A 1AY. Tel: (020) 7438 4700.

KEEPING RECORDS

Contributions Agency. The government agency responsible for collecting National Insurance payments from employers and the self-employed. See your local phone book for telephone number and address.

Customs and Excise, New King's Beam House, 22 Upper Ground, London SE1 9PJ. Tel: (020) 7620 1313. Or see your local phone book. The organisation responsible for collecting and refunding VAT payments.

Department of Social Security, Alexander Fleming House, Elephant and Castle, London SE1 6BY. Tel: (020) 7972 2000. Or see your local phone book.

DSS Leaflet Unit, PO Box 21, Stanmore, Middlesex HA7 1AY. Tel: 0800 393 539.

Inland Revenue, Somerset House, Strand, London WC2R 1LB. Tel: (020) 7438 6622. Or see your local phone book. The organisation responsible for assessing income tax, corporation tax, advance corporation tax, capital gains tax, inheritance and other taxes. Collection is undertaken by a separate organisation, The Collector of Taxes based in Yorkshire.

Please bear in mind that organisations can, and frequently do, relocate and change their phone numbers. You may need to refer to the last local telephone directory or to dial '192' for directory enquiries.

More Business Books to Help You

STARTING A BUSINESS

Becoming a Consultant, Susan Nash (How To Books, 1999).

Be Your Own Boss, British Telecom Guide.

The Business of Freelancing, Graham Jones (BFP Jones 1987).

Buying a Franchise, Phil Stone (How To Books, 2000).

Starting a Business From Home, Graham Jones (How To Books, 4th edition, 1999).

The Wyvern Business Library, Wyvern House, 7 The Business Park, Ely, Cambridgeshire CB7 4JW. Suppliers of a wide range of business books, available through mail order.

Getting Started, R Rhodes (Kogan Page, 1995).

How to be an Entrepreneur, I Phillipson (Kogan Page, 1993).

The First 12 Months, D Bangs (Kogan Page, 1993).

Working for Yourself, G Golzen (Kogan Page, 1995).

A *Guide to Working from Home*, British Telecom Guide.

Running Your Own Business – Planning for Success (Department of Employment).

Small Business Digest, quarterly (National Westminster Bank).

Small Business Insurance Advice File (Association of British Insurers).

Sources of Free Business Information, Michael Brooks (Kogan Page, 1986).

Start Up and go with NatWest (National Westminster Bank).

Starting Up Your Own Business, 3i (Investors in Industry).

Starting Your Business (Lloyds Bank).

Starting Your Own Business – the Practical Steps (Department of Employment).

Starting Your Own Business (Barclays Bank).

Starting a Small Business, Alan and Deborah Fowler (Warner Books).

Starting Up, G Jones (Pitman Publishing, 1991).

Swim With the Sharks, Harvey Mackay (Warner Books).

101 Great Money Making Ideas, Mark Hempshell (Northcote House).

Franchising: A Practical Guide for Franchisors and Franchisees, I Maitland (Mercury, 1991).

Setting Up a Limited Company, Robert Browning (How To Books, 2nd edition, 1999).

Taking up a Franchise, Matthew Record (How To Books, 1999).

ORGANISING YOURSELF

Conquering the Paper Pile-Up, Stephanie Culp (Writer's Digest Books, Cincinnati, 1990).
Getting Things Done: The ABC of Time Management, Edwin C Biss (Warner Publications).
Running Your Office, Margaret Korving (BBC, 1989).
The Seven Keys to Superefficiency, Winston Fletcher (Sidgwick & Jackson, 1986).
10-Minute Time and Stress Management, Dr David Lewis (Piatkus).
Managing Growth, M Bennett (Pitman Publishing, 1991).
Small Business Survival, R Bennett (Pitman Publishing, 1991).
Managing Your Time, Julie Amos (How To Books, 1998).

BUSINESS PLANNING

The Business Planner: A Complete Guide to Raising Finance, I Maitland (Butterworth Heinemann, 1992).
The Business Plan Workbook, Colin and Paul Barrow (Kogan Page Ltd, 1988).
Business Planning & Development, a Practical Guide, Bill Elsom (First Class Publishing, Doncaster).
Preparing a Winning Business Plan, Matthew Record (How To Books, 3rd edition, 2000).
How To Prepare a Business Plan (2nd edition), Edward Blackwell (Kogan Page Publishers, 1993).
The Perfect Business Plan, Ron Johnson (Century Business, 1993).

KEEPING FINANCIAL CONTROL

The Barclays Guide to Financial Management for the Small Business Peter Wilson (Blackwell Publishers, 1990).
Business Cash Books Made Easy, M Pullen (Kogan Page, 1992).
Budgeting for the Non-Financial Manager, I Maitland (Pitman Publishing, 1995).
Financial Control, D Irwin (Pitman Publishing, 1991).
Budgetary Control in the Small Company, 3i (Investors in Industry).
Managing Your Business Accounts, Peter Taylor (How To Books, 5th edition, 1999).
Cash Flows & Budgeting Made Easy, Peter Taylor (How To Books, 3rd edition, 2000).
Cashflow & How to Improve It, Leon Hopkins (Kogan Page, 1993).
Mastering Book-Keeping, Peter Marshall (How To Books, 4th edition, 1999).

BUSINESS COMPUTING

I Hate Buying a Computer, Jim Felici (Que).
Buy a PC, Mike James (I/O Press).
Beginners Guide to the PC, McKellan and Waixel (Kuma Books).
Ten Minute Guide to the Internet & World Wide Web, Galen Grimes (QUE).
Teach Yourself the Internet in 24 Hours, Noel Estabrook (SamsNet).
Doing Business on the Internet, Graham Jones (How To Books, 1997).

MARKETING & PROMOTION

Effective Negotiating, C Robinson (Kogan Page, 1995).
Don't Get Mad, Write, Bruce West (Kogan Page).
High Income Consulting, Tom Lambert (Nicholas Brealey).
How To Increase Sales by Telephone, Alfred Tack (The Windmill Press, Surrey, 1971).
How to Promote Your Own Business, Jim Dudley.
Writing a Press Release, Peter Bartram (How to Books, 3rd edition, 1999).
Writing a Report, John Bowden (How To Books, 5th edition, 2000).
The Language of Success, BT Booklet.
101 Ways to Get More Business, Timothy R V Foster (Kogan Page).
The Secrets of Effective Direct Mail, John Fraser-Robinson (McGraw-Hill, London 1989).
The Secrets of Successful Copywriting, Patrick Quinn (Heinemann, London).
The Secrets of Successful Low-Budget Advertising, Patrick Quinn (Heinemann, London 1987).
Seductive Selling, Kit Sadgrove (Kogan Press).
Total Confidence, Philipa Davies (Piatkus).
Write Right, A Desk Draw Digest of Punctuation, Grammar and Style, Jan Vernolia (David & Charles, London 1982).
Writing to Sell, The Complete Guide to Copywriting for Business, Kit Sadgrove (Robert Hale, London 1991).
Writing to Win, Mel Lewis (McGraw-Hill, London 1987).
The Power of Persuasion (Wyvern Business Library, 1992).
Prospecting for Customers (Wyvern Business Library, 1994).
How to Plan Direct Mail, I Maitland (Cassell, 1995).
How to Plan Press Advertising, I Maitland (Cassell, 1995).
Making Direct Mail Work, Peter Arnold (How To Books, 1999).
How to Plan Radio Advertising, I Maitland (Cassell, 1995).
How to Sell a Service, Malcolm McDonald and John Leppart (Heinemann, 1986).
How to Win Customers, Heinz Goldman (Pan, London 1980).
Successful Marketing for the Small Business, Dave Patten (Kogan Page).
Successful Negotiation, R Maddux (Kogan Page, 1988).
Selling, P Allen (Pitman Publishing, 1991).

TAKING ON STAFF

Getting a Result, I Maitland (Institute of Personnel and Development, 1994).
Managing Performance Reviews, Nigel Hunt (How To Books, 4th edition, 1999).
Managing Through People, John Humphries (How To Books, 3rd edition, 1998).
How to Recruit, I Maitland, (Gower, 1992).
Managing Staff, I Maitland (Cassell, 1995).
Motivating People, I Maitland (Institute of Personnel and Development, 1995).
Recruiting for the Future, I Maitland (Cassell, 1995).
Modern Employment Law, M Whinchup (Butterworth Heinemann, 1995).
Managing Individual Performance, Kieron Baldwin (How To Books, 1999).

USING PROFESSIONAL ADVISERS

Dealing with Your Bank, Brian Cain (How To Books, 1997).
Getting Value from Professional Advisers, C Standish (Kogan Page, 1993).
Why You Need a Chartered Accountant (Institute of Chartered Accountants).

UNDERSTANDING BUSINESS LAW

Computers and the Law, David Bainbridge (Pitman, 1990).
Law for the Small Business, Patricia Clayton (Kogan Page, 1991).
A Step by Step Guide to Planning Permission for Small Businesses available from your local authority planning department.
Your Business and the Law, John Harries (Oyez Longman).
Health and Safety, V Broadhurst (Pitman Publishing, 1991).
Heath and Safety Law, J Stranks (Pitman Publishing, 1994).
Law for Small Businesses, A Holmes, R Evans, C Wright, S Wright (Pitman Publishing, 1991).

PAYING TAX

Coping with Self Assessment, J Whiteley (How To Books, 4th edition, 2000).
How to Cut Your Tax Bills, G Thornton (Kogan Page, 1995).
Paying Less Tax, John Whiteley (How To Books, 2nd edition, 2000).
Tax for the Self-employed (Allied-Dunbar Money Guide), David Williams (Longman, 1990).
Taxman Tactics, How to play by the rules – and win, Stephen Courtney (Sidgwick and Jackson, 1990).
Taxation, T Docherty (Pitman Publishing, 1994).

Taxes on Business, K Armstrong (Kogan Page, 1994).
Understanding VAT, W Lovell (Pitman Publishing, 1991).
The VAT Guide (HM Customs and Excise).

BUSINESS PERIODICALS

Home Run, 'The action guide to working successfully for yourself.' Active Information, 79 Black Lion Lane, London W6 9BG. Tel: (0181) 846 9244.

OwnBase: The Newsletter for Home-based Workers, 68 First Avenue, Bush Hill Park, Enfield EN1 1BN.

Exchange & Mart. Available weekly (Thursdays) from newsagents. Includes many business opportunities, services, and goods for sale.

Daltons Weekly. Featuring property, business and investment opportunities.

Managing Your Business. Glossy magazine published by Chase Communications, 66-68 Pentonville Road, London N1 9HS. Tel: (0171) 837 9977.

Your Business: The Guide to Small Business Success. Illustrated business magazine published by Merlin Publications Ltd, Unit 14, Hove Business Centre, Fonthill Road, Hove, East Sussex BN3 6HA. Tel: (01273) 888992

INTERNET

The Complete Idiot's Guide to the Internet, Peter Kent (Prentice Hall Europe).
How to Activate Your Web Site, Bob Algie (Ziff Davis, 1998).
Doing Business on the Internet, Graham Jones (How To Books).
Internet in an Hour, Don Mayo (DDC Publishing, 1998).
How to Use the Internet, Mark E Walker (Ziff Davies, 4th edition).
Doing Business on the World Wide Web, Marni C Patterson (Ziff Davies).
Teleworking Explained, M Gray, N Hodson and G Gordon (John Wiley & Sons)
Teleworking in Brief, Mike Johnson (Butterworth/Heinemann).
Using the Internet, Graham Jones (How To Books, 3rd edition, 1999).

Index